First published in 2005 by Bardfield Press

Bardfield Press is an imprint of
Miles Kelly Publishing
Bardfield Centre, Great Bardfield,
Essex, CM7 4SL

British Library Cataloguing-in-Publication Data.
A catalogue record for this book is available from the British Library

ISBN 1-84236-543-6

2 4 6 8 10 9 7 5 3 1

Editorial Director: Belinda Gallagher

Project Manager: Lisa Clayden

Production Manager: Estela Boulton

Designer: Helen Weller

Questions: Brian Williams

Cartoons and design concept: Mark Davis, Mackerel Ltd

Contact us by email:
info@mileskelly.net

Visit us on the web:
www.mileskelly.net

Printed in China

Contents

How to use this book

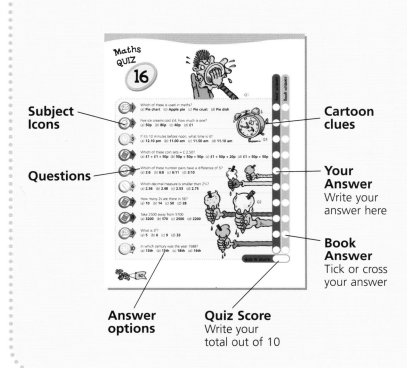

Subject Icons

Questions

Answer options

Quiz Score
Write your total out of 10

Cartoon clues

Your Answer
Write your answer here

Book Answer
Tick or cross your answer

Your book is split into four subject sections each with 28 quizzes, each quiz contains ten multiple-choice questions. There are six subject categories in each section for you to choose from. Simply write your answers in pencil in the answer panel. Turn to the answers at the back of the book to check your answers. Rub out your answers and try again! You can chart your progress by using the score sheets at the end of each section.

English

Key to subject icons

 Books and writers

 Word meanings

 Myths and legends

 Spellings

 Sounds and rhymes

 Grammar

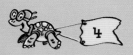

English QUIZ

1

Q1

Your answer   Book answer

 1 A pirate's sword is a … what?
(a) **Windlass** (b) **Cutlass** (c) **Cutlet** (d) **Cutlery**

 2 Which pantomime hero sells the family cow for a bag of beans?
(a) **Jack** (b) **Jill** (c) **Simple Simon** (d) **Mother Goose**

 3 Sounds like a smell and a US coin?
(a) **Scent/Cent** (b) **Tinge/Fringe** (c) **Butt/Nut** (d) **Pong/Gong**

 4 Use this animal to hit a ball:
(a) **Cat** (b) **Bat** (c) **Bear** (d) **Seal**

Q2

 5 Twinkle, twinkle, little …
(a) **Star** (b) **Moon** (c) **Sun** (d) **Planet**

 6 Another word for a horse-drawn cart:
(a) **Flagon** (b) **Wagon** (c) **Dragon** (d) **Saigon**

 7 Add -er to make a drinking cup:
(a) **Bill..** (b) **Boot..** (c) **Beak..** (d) **Belt..**

 8 A verb meaning to pull out:
(a) **Extract** (b) **Explain** (c) **Exercise** (d) **Exhaust**

 9 Which of these is a vowel?
(a) **E** (b) **G** (c) **H** (d) **M**

Q4

 10 The plural of ox is … what?
(a) **Oxes** (b) **Oxs** (c) **Oxen** (d) **Ox**

Quiz 1 score

5

English QUIZ 2

Q6

1 What's another word meaning 'sad'?
(a) **Cross** (b) **Sorrowful** (c) **Bad** (d) **Glad**

2 What part of speech is Bill in 'Bill ate quickly'?
(a) **Verb** (b) **Adjective** (c) **Proper noun** (d) **Adverb**

3 In which pantomime do Wishee Washee and Widow Twankey appear?
(a) **Aladdin** (b) **Babes in the Wood** (c) **Cinderella** (d) **Dick Whittington**

4 Which abbreviation means 'rest in peace'?
(a) **RIP** (b) **VIP** (c) **RSVP** (d) **PTO**

5 Something you'd cross on a country walk?
(a) **Mile** (b) **File** (c) **Stile** (d) **Tile**

Q3

6 Who was Robin Hood's outsized companion?
(a) **Big Jake** (b) **Giant Haystacks** (c) **Mighty Man** (d) **Little John**

7 What part of speech is slowly in 'She walked slowly'?
(a) **Noun** (b) **Adverb** (c) **Verb** (d) **Preposition**

8 Which Shakespeare play is about a Scot whose wife drives him to murder?
(a) **Macbeth** (b) **Hamlet** (c) **Richard III** (d) **Othello**

9 The first book of the Bible:
(a) **Acts** (b) **Matthew** (c) **Psalms** (d) **Genesis**

10 These are in the chromosomes of everybody: Q8
(a) **Genes** (b) **Jeans** (c) **Beans** (d) **Seams**

Quiz 2 score

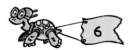

English QUIZ

3

Q1

		Your answer	Book answer

 1 Which Shakespeare play is about a Danish prince?
(a) **Hamlet**   (b) **Henry V**   (c) **Romeo and Juliet**   (d) **King Lear**

 2 Place where metal is melted and shaped:
(a) **Laundry**   (b) **Boundary**   (c) **Dairy**   (d) **Foundry**

 3 Which of these would you play?
(a) **Flute**   (b) **Loot**   (c) **Boot**   (d) **Cute**

Q3

 4 Which abbreviation means 'please reply'?
(a) **RSVP**   (b) **OBE**   (c) **DFC**   (d) **BBC**

 5 Who wrote about the BFG?
(a) **Roald Dahl**   (b) **J.K. Rowling**   (c) **Enid Blyton**   (d) **Richmal Crompton**

 6 What does an arachnophobe hate?
(a) **Toothbrushes**   (b) **Spiders**   (c) **The dark**   (d) **Fireworks**

 7 Which of these is a storybook elephant?
(a) **Spot**   (b) **Orlando**   (c) **Kanga**   (d) **Babar**

Q6

 8 Where would you find props and flies?
(a) **On a boat**   (b) **In a theatre**   (c) **In a zoo**   (d) **In a laundry**

 9 Sunil has a bike: the bike is …
(a) **Sunils**   (b) **Sunils'**   (c) **Sunil's**   (d) **Suniles**

 10 The opposite of timid:
(a) **Scared**   (b) **Greedy**   (c) **Bold**   (d) **Huge**

Quiz 3 score

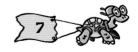

7

English QUIZ

4

Q1

 1 In which book by Charles Dickens does Scrooge appear?
(a) **A Christmas Carol** (b) **Oliver Twist** (c) **Hard Times** (d) **David Copperfield**

 2 Someone who puts on a stage show is a …?
(a) **Protester** (b) **Preparer** (c) **Producer** (d) **Projector**

 3 A kind of poem:
(a) **Sonnet** (b) **Sonata** (c) **Settee** (d) **Sofa**

 4 Which word rhymes with 'dove'?
(a) **Move** (b) **Love** (c) **Cave** (d) **Dive**

Q6

 5 A word that means 'eating too much':
(a) **Gluttony** (b) **Laziness** (c) **Sloth** (d) **Jealousy**

 6 The boy who never grew up?
(a) **William** (b) **Peter Pan** (c) **Oliver Twist** (d) **Charlie Bucket**

 7 What kind of animal was Black Beauty?
(a) **Cat** (b) **Dog** (c) **Gorilla** (d) **Horse**

 8 What do we call a group of farm geese?
(a) **Gaggle** (b) **Herd** (c) **Coven** (d) **Clutch**

 9 Which word fills the gap: We … going on holiday?
(a) **Enter** (b) **Enjoy** (c) **Often** (d) **Kind**

I Love You

Q4

 10 The one-legged pirate of *Treasure Island*:
(a) **Long John Silver** (b) **Captain Kidd** (c) **Blackbeard** (d) **Benbow**

Quiz 4 score

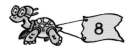

English QUIZ

5

Your answer | Book answer

1 A fruit and a colour:
(a) **Lime** (b) **Pawpaw** (c) **Grape** (d) **Gooseberry**

2 A word meaning 'fear of being shut in':
(a) **Hysteria** (b) **Vertigo** (c) **Claustrophobia** (d) **Nausea**

3 How do you spell what birds do in trees at night?
(a) **Rust** (b) **Roost** (c) **Roast** (d) **Rewst**

4 What do we call a male sheep?   Q7
(a) **Ram** (b) **Bull** (c) **Dog** (d) **Stallion**

5 Where did Toad live?
(a) **Mole End** (b) **Badger's Mount** (c) **The Willows** (d) **Toad Hall**

6 Complete the book title: *The ... Steps*
(a) **Slippery** (b) **39** (c) **1001** (d) **Steep**

7 Which word could be a noun and a verb?
(a) **Elephant** (b) **Saucepan** (c) **Flower** (d) **Shirt**

8 Find the consonant:
(a) **E** (b) **I** (c) **T** (d) **A**   Q1

9 What is the plural of country?
(a) **Country** (b) **Countries** (c) **Countrys** (d) **Countryes**

10 Which word means 'horrible to look at'?
(a) **Repulsive** (b) **Refreshing** (c) **Rebellious** (d) **Restored**

Quiz 5 score

English QUIZ

6

		Your answer	Book answer
1	Which group was written about by Enid Blyton? (a) **Famous Five** (b) **Simple Six** (c) **Fab Four** (d) **Terrible Two**	○	○
2	Which of these was a Scottish writer? (a) **Tolstoy** (b) **Dickens** (c) **Twain** (d) **Burns**	○	○
3	A person walking on foot is a …? (a) **Pedestrian** (b) **Bystander** (c) **Terrestrial** (d) **Motorist**	○	○
4	A test at school or college: (a) **Examination** (b) **Exhibition** (c) **Explanation** (d) **Explosion**	○	○
5	Make an adverb from happy: (a) **Happymost** (b) **Happiness** (c) **Be happy** (d) **Happily**	○	○
6	Jim was very tired; he was … what? (a) **Exasperated** (b) **Exhausted** (c) **Excited** (d) **Ecstatic**	○	○
7	One mouse, ten … what? (a) **Mouses** (b) **Meese** (c) **Mices** (d) **Mice**	○	○
8	What is the punctuation mark called at the end of this sentence? (a) **Full stop** (b) **Exclamation mark** (c) **Question mark** (d) **Colon**	○	○
9	Complete this sentence to make sense: 'Books are …' (a) **Good to eat** (b) **Electric** (c) **Hot to handle** (d) **Made of paper**	○	○
10	This tells you how to cook a meal: (a) **Recipe** (b) **Receipt** (c) **Record** (d) **Remedy**	○	○

Q10

Q9

Q7

Quiz 6 score

English QUIZ

7

 1 Which of these is not a comparative?
(a) **Cheaper** (b) **Bigger** (c) **Ugly** (d) **Brighter**

 2 What is Bilbo and Frodo's surname?
(a) **Goggins** (b) **Higgins** (c) **Baggins** (d) **Hawkins**

 3 If something happens every day it happens:
(a) **Daily** (b) **Weekly** (c) **Monthly** (d) **Yearly**

 4 Another word for bucket:
(a) **Pile** (b) **Pole** (c) **Pill** (d) **Pail**

 5 The plural of class is …?
(a) **Class** (b) **Clases** (c) **Classes** (d) **Classy**

 6 Which word is not a meal?
(a) **Snack** (b) **Sandwich** (c) **Supper** (d) **Sofa**

 7 Which spelling would you find in school?
(a) **Teecher** (b) **Teacher** (c) **Teetcher** (d) **Teasher**

 8 Complete the Raymond Briggs book title: *Fungus the …?*
(a) **Farmer** (b) **Toadstool** (c) **Bogeyman** (d) **Snowman**

 9 Which word rhymes with flower?
(a) **Shower** (b) **Tour** (c) **Flier** (d) **Boot**

 10 As … as a doornail *(proverb)*:
(a) **Hard** (b) **Deaf** (c) **Silent** (d) **Dead**

Q8

Q4

Q6

Your answer

Book answer

Quiz 7 score

11

English QUIZ

8

Q6

	Your answer	Book answer

 1 A book full of information and facts:
(a) **Diary**   (b) **Encyclopedia**   (c) **Dictionary**   (d) **Atlas**

 2 Who wrote *Oliver Twist*?
(a) **Charles Dickens**   (b) **Jane Austen**   (c) **William Shakespeare**   (d) **Daniel Defoe**

Q2

 3 Which is correct here for more than one apple?
(a) **Apple**   (b) **Apples**   (c) **Apple's**   (d) **Applemore**

 4 Which of these ends a sentence?
(a) **Full stop**   (b) **Colon**   (c) **Semi-colon**   (d) **Comma**

 5 If someone has the letters FRCS after their name, what are they?
(a) **Footballer**   (b) **Musician**   (c) **Surgeon**   (d) **Astronaut**

 6 Fill in the missing word in this book title: *Dr Jekyll and …*
(a) **Mr Hyde**   (b) **Dr Who**   (c) **Mrs Brown**   (d) **The Witch**

 7 We live … an old home (what word fits best)?
(a) **In**   (b) **Before**   (c) **Out**   (d) **Round**

 8 A place where students live and work:
(a) **Underground**   (b) **Universe**   (c) **Untidy**   (d) **University**

9 Little Miss Muffet sat on a …
(a) **Cushion**   (b) **Toadstool**   (c) **Tuffet**   (d) **Tussock**   Q9

 10 Someone who works in a hospital:
(a) **Nurse**   (b) **North**   (c) **Nourish**   (d) **Nut**

Quiz 8 score

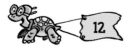

English QUIZ

9

Q3

 1 Spell a word that means 'brainy':
(a) **Untellijent** (b) **Intellyjent** (c) **Intilligent** (d) **Intelligent**

 2 Which word rhymes with 'shiny'?
(a) **Tinny** (b) **Tiny** (c) **Slimy** (d) **Grimy**

 3 Which hero shot an apple off his son's head?
(a) **Robin Hood** (b) **Spiderman** (c) **El Cid** (d) **William Tell**

Q5

 4 Which horselike mythical creature had one horn?
(a) **Centaur** (b) **Dragon** (c) **Griffin** (d) **Unicorn**

Q8

 5 What do we call a lot of fish?
(a) **Shoal** (b) **Bowl** (c) **Platoon** (d) **Herd**

 6 What is a book full of maps called?
(a) **Dictionary** (b) **Directory** (c) **Atlas** (d) **Encyclopedia**

 7 What was Mary Poppins' job?
(a) **Children's nanny** (b) **Teacher** (c) **Shopkeeper** (d) **Chimney sweep**

 8 Which is wrong here?
(a) **Five frogs** (b) **Four cats** (c) **Ten beetle's** (d) **Six ships**

 9 Which spelling is correct here?
(a) **Whynoceros** (b) **Rhinoceros** (c) **Raynosheros** (d) **Ryenosharos**

 10 Hickory dickory dock – where did the mouse run?
(a) **Into their hole** (b) **Up the pole** (c) **Up the clock** (d) **Under the rock**

Quiz 9 score

13

English QUIZ

10

Q2

 1 To fire a bullet, add s:
(a) _**hort**   (b) _**hoot**   (c) _**have**   (d) _**hirt**

2 Who rubbed a magic lamp?
(a) **Buttons**   (b) **Dick Whittington**   (c) **Aladdin**   (d) **Peter Pan**

 3 Captain of a ship:
(a) **Scooter**   (b) **Skipper**   (c) **Shopper**   (d) **Slipper**

 4 Which of these means to bear flowers?
(a) **Sprout**   (b) **Grow**   (c) **Bloom**   (d) **Seed**

5 Who in Greek myth sailed with the Argonauts?
(a) **Neptune**   (b) **Helen**   (c) **Jason**   (d) **Nelson**

Q5

 6 Only one of these is correct, which one is it?
(a) **Kellys' shoes**   (b) **Kelly's shoes**   (c) **Kellys shoe's**   (d) **Kellys shoes'**

 7 Which word is a verb here?
(a) **Run**   (b) **Giraffe**   (c) **Slowly**   (d) **Terrible**

 8 In the garden, good for planting:
(a) **Toil**   (b) **Foil**   (c) **Oil**   (d) **Soil**

Q8

 9 Means 'frequently':
(a) **Often**   (b) **Always**   (c) **Sometimes**   (d) **Never**

 10 Which spelling is correct for this day of the week?
(a) **Whensday**   (b) **Wensday**   (c) **Wednesday**   (d) **Wennsday**

Quiz 10 score

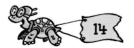

English QUIZ

11

Q2

1 A word that means 'cross':
(a) **Hungry** (b) **Angry** (c) **Empty** (d) **Early**

2 What we do in elections:
(a) **Voat** (b) **Voot** (c) **Vowt** (d) **Vote**

3 The opposite of open:
(a) **Closed** (b) **Clothed** (c) **Clean** (d) **Cling**

4 Which of these would you find in the kitchen?
(a) **Paint** (b) **Spade** (c) **Spoon** (d) **Parrot**

Q4

5 Which colour rhymes best with Bean?
(a) **Blue** (b) **Green** (c) **Red** (d) **Black**

6 Pick out the vowel here:
(a) **L** (b) **E** (c) **G** (d) **R**

7 Which is the capital letter in this group?
(a) **y** (b) **B** (c) **d** (d) **e**

Q8

8 A large fish:
(a) **Tiger** (b) **Tomcat** (c) **Turtle** (d) **Tuna**

9 A book of the Bible:
(a) **Acts** (b) **Deeds** (c) **Sayings** (d) **Events**

10 Which of these authors writes poetry?
(a) **Jacqueline Wilson** (b) **Anne Fine** (c) **Philip Pullman** (d) **Ted Hughes**

Quiz 11 score

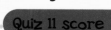
15

English QUIZ

12

Q6

		Your answer	Book answer

? **1** Which of these are not cattle?
(a) **Oxen** (b) **Bullocks** (c) **Heifers** (d) **Stallions**

2 Complete the sentence: 'The sky is …'
(a) **Green** (b) **Blue** (c) **Sticky** (d) **Greasy**

♪ **3** Little Jack Horner sat in the … what?
(a) **Haystack** (b) **Pigsty** (c) **Water** (d) **Corner**

? **4** Vehicle + animal = floor covering:
(a) **Garden** (b) **Carpet** (c) **Cartoon** (d) **Cartwheel**

Q3

5 Which spelling is correct for a large land mass?
(a) **Continent** (b) **Country** (c) **Constant** (d) **Capital**

6 Which brothers told *The Goose Girl* and other fairy stories?
(a) **Grimm** (b) **Smith** (c) **Dumas** (d) **James**

7 To make a smoothing tool, add the letter p:
(a) **_lait** (b) **_lane** (c) **_lant** (d) **_late**

8 The pen that swings:
(a) **Pentagon** (b) **Penguin** (c) **Pendulum** (d) **Peninsula**

9 What is the penultimate letter of the alphabet?
(a) **Y** (b) **Z** (c) **A** (d) **M**

Q8

10 Which book hero got to run a Chocolate Factory?
(a) **William** (b) **Charlie** (c) **Billy** (d) **Sam**

Quiz 12 score

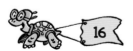

English QUIZ

13

Q6

Your answer **Book answer**

1 A kind of dog:
(a) **Poodle**   (b) **Paddle**   (c) **Puddle**   (d) **Puzzle**

2 What does a philatelist collect?
(a) **Coins**   (b) **Stamps**   (c) **Cars**   (d) **Postcards**

3 A kind of teacher: which spelling is correct?
(a) **Professer**   (b) **Professor**   (c) **Profesor**   (d) **Proffessor**

4 In which forest did Robin Hood live?
(a) **Sherwood**   (b) **Arden**   (c) **New**   (d) **Epping**

Q1

5 Which word rhymes with beaver?
(a) **Feather**   (b) **Ever**   (c) **Tether**   (d) **Fever**

6 Who was not at the Mad Hatter's Teaparty?
(a) **Alice**   (b) **Dormouse**   (c) **March Hare**   (d) **Cheshire Cat**

7 Which word best completes this sentence: Mrs Smith met her …?
(a) **Handbag**   (b) **Husband**   (c) **Hobby**   (d) **Hoop**

8 Who is headmaster at Hogwarts?
(a) **Jeremiah Creakle**   (b) **Hagrid**   (c) **Dumbledore**   (d) **Thwackum**

9 What is the plural of bus?
(a) **Bus**   (b) **Buses**   (c) **Busses**   (d) **Buss**   Q6

10 What's another word meaning 'quickly'?
(a) **Swiftly**   (b) **Clumsily**   (c) **Badly**   (d) **Cheerfully**

Quiz 13 score

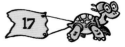

17

English QUIZ

14

Q5

Your answer

Book answer

1 Something to eat:
(a) **Poster** (b) **Pasta** (c) **Painting** (d) **Pottery**

2 Which people told stories about Valhalla?
(a) **Hindus** (b) **Chinese** (c) **Vikings** (d) **Native Americans**

3 Female kind of duke:
(a) **Dukeness** (b) **She-duke** (c) **Duchess** (d) **Dukemam**

Q1

4 A book in which cabin boy Jim Hawkins appears:
(a) **Stig of the Dump** (b) **Lord of the Flies** (c) **Treasure Island** (d) **Black Beauty**

5 Where did Jack and Jill go *(nursery rhyme)*?
(a) **Down the lane** (b) **Up the hill** (c) **To the shops** (d) **To the fair**

6 Which of these spellings is correct?
(a) **Comepooter** (b) **Komputer** (c) **Computer** (d) **Commpewtah**

7 Who was King Arthur's wizard?
(a) **Maud Moonshine** (b) **Saruman** (c) **Merlin** (d) **Hecate**

8 Unscramble the letters to make part of a book: Q7
(a) **GEPA** (b) **TEAP** (c) **TAES** (d) **GTEA**

9 Which title is correct for this book by Chaucer?
(a) **London Legends** (b) **Romford Rhymes** (c) **Canterbury Tales** (d) **Stoke Stories**

10 Which word rhymes with 'teeth'?
(a) **Breath** (b) **Heath** (c) **Booth** (d) **Greet**

Quiz 14 score

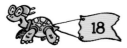

English QUIZ

15

 1 Something to keep you cool: Q1
(a) **Fin** (b) **Fun** (c) **Fen** (d) **Fan**

 2 What is the name of Captain Nemo's submarine?
(a) **Nautilus** (b) **Enterprise** (c) **White Shark** (d) **Beagle**

 3 Whose travels took him to a land of little people?
(a) **Dick Turpin** (b) **Tom Thumb** (c) **Gulliver** (d) **Willy Wonka**

 4 Which of these might not be on a ship?
(a) **Sailor** (b) **Sail** (c) **Tailor** (d) **Anchor**

 5 Spell an insect that buzzes:
(a) **Fly** (b) **Fish** (c) **Flea** (d) **Flag**

 6 American word for rubbish:
(a) **Trash** (b) **Tissue** (c) **Tramp** (d) **Treat**

 7 The fifth day of the week: Q3
(a) **Monday** (b) **Thursday** (c) **Wednesday** (d) **Tuesday**

 8 Plural of wolf:
(a) **Wolf** (b) **Wolfes** (c) **Wolves** (d) **Wolffes**

 9 The grain from which we make bread:
(a) **Wheat** (b) **Cheat** (c) **Heat** (d) **Meat**

 10 To blow up a balloon means to:
(a) **Eat it** (b) **Inflate it** (c) **Remove it** (d) **Omit it**

Quiz 15 score

Q2

English QUIZ

16

Q10

Your answer

Book answer

1 Another word for silly:
(a) **Feeble** (b) **Friendly** (c) **Foolish** (d) **Fat**

2 The future tense of 'to run'?
(a) **I run** (b) **I will run** (c) **I ran** (d) **I have run**

3 What insult does Draco Malfoy call Hermione Granger?
(a) **Hairyface** (b) **Weirdo** (c) **Pimples** (d) **Mudblood**

4 A coloured stick to draw with:
(a) **Crayon** (b) **Iron** (c) **Nylon** (d) **Lion**

Q4

5 How do you spell the name of a person who serves you in a restaurant?
(a) **Waiter** (b) **Water** (c) **Wheyter** (d) **Waytar**

6 The noise a sheep makes:
(a) **Sleet** (b) **Bleat** (c) **Great** (d) **Meat**

7 As firm as a … what:
(a) **Sponge** (b) **Jelly** (c) **Ice cream** (d) **Rock**

Q9

8 A group of deer:
(a) **Pack** (b) **Litter** (c) **Herd** (d) **School**

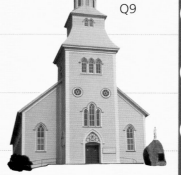

9 How do you spell this place of worship?
(a) **Shurch** (b) **Church** (c) **Lurch** (d) **Kurchl**

10 What kind of creature is Dracula?
(a) **Dragon** (b) **Vampire** (c) **Witch** (d) **Robot**

Quiz 16 score

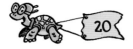

English QUIZ

17

Q6

1 As tough as old … what?
(a) **Chewing gum**   (b) **Boots**   (c) **Bacon**   (d) **Bread**

2 Someone who likes making jokes is a:
(a) **Juggler**   (b) **Jumper**   (c) **Joker**   (d) **Jockey**

3 How do you spell this word meaning a group of sheep?
(a) **Flock**   (b) **Floock**   (c) **Phlock**   (d) **Throng**

Q1

4 Means a boat and to bump into:
(a) **Bash**   (b) **Barge**   (c) **Bulge**   (d) **Bingo**

5 Which is the past tense of the verb 'to sleep'?
(a) **Sleeping**   (b) **Slept**   (c) **Will sleep**   (d) **Will be sleeping**

6 How many blackbirds were baked in a pie?
(a) **Four and Twenty**   (b) **Five dozen**   (c) **Two**   (d) **Fifty**

7 Which word means 'two times'?
(a) **Once**   (b) **Twice**   (c) **Several**   (d) **Lots of**

Q2

8 Which is correct here *(means ' I went in a plane')*?
(a) **I flew**   (b) **I flyed**   (c) **I flowed**   (d) **I flewed**

9 Which Greek hero had to do 12 Tasks or Labours?
(a) **Achilles**   (b) **Perseus**   (c) **Hercules**   (d) **Alexander**

10 'The hair of Jenny' – which is correct here?
(a) **Jennys hair**   (b) **Jenny's hair**   (c) **Jennys' hair**   (d) **J'ennys hair**

Quiz 17 score

English QUIZ

18

Q10

Your answer | Book answer

 1 Which spelling is correct?
(a) **Dikshunary** (b) **Dikshonerry** (c) **Dictionary** (d) **Dickshunari**

 2 And what does the above word mean?
(a) **Book of maps** (b) **Book of words** (c) **Phone book** (d) **Cookery book**

 3 Which of these is the infinitive of the verb?
(a) **Doing** (b) **To do** (c) **Done** (d) **Did**

Q6

 4 To climb up something:
(a) **Meet** (b) **Mint** (c) **Moult** (d) **Mount**

 5 Another word for a thief:
(a) **Beggar** (b) **Prisoner** (c) **Robber** (d) **Fighter**

 6 Which nursery character blew his horn?
(a) **Peter Piper** (b) **Little Boy Blue** (c) **Jack Horner** (b) **Humpty Dumpty**

 7 Which word describes a dog?
(a) **Canine** (b) **Feline** (c) **Bovine** (d) **Equine**

 8 'The book belonging to Tom': which is correct here?
(a) **Toms book** (b) **Tom's book** (c) **Book's Tom** (d) **Toms' book**

 9 Which of these ends a question?
(a) **?** (b) **"** (c) **!** (d) **(**

Q5

 10 In which book does Man Friday leave his footprint on an island?
(a) **Robinson Crusoe** (b) **Lost Weekend** (c) **Treasure Island** (d) **Matilda**

Quiz 18 score

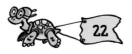

English QUIZ

19

 1 Means 'as muddy as can be':
(a) **Muddiest** (b) **Muddy** (c) **Muddier** (d) **Mud**

 2 Which has the apostrophe in the right place?
(a) **Must' not** (b) **Mustn't** (c) **Must'not** (d) **Must'nt**

 3 A bird and to complain:
(a) **Whinge** (b) **Grumble** (c) **Moan** (d) **Grouse**

 4 France is famous for … wine and cheese *(fill the gap)*:
(a) **Its** (b) **Their** (c) **Ours** (d) **Yours**

 5 Which of these is an adjective?
(a) **Slowly** (b) **Clever** (c) **Classroom** (d) **Book**

Q3

 6 What is the opposite of shallow?
(a) **Wide** (b) **Long** (c) **Thin** (d) **Deep**

Q9

 7 What do we call a group of dolphins?
(a) **School** (b) **Class** (c) **Band** (d) **Gaggle**

 8 The past tense of 'I run':
(a) **I ran** (b) **I run** (c) **I runned** (d) **I ranned**

 9 Which word rhymes with cherry?
(a) **Chair** (b) **Bear** (c) **Berry** (d) **Chilly**

 10 Who or what does a misanthropist hate?
(a) **Everybody** (b) **Animals** (c) **Ants** (d) **Fog**

Q7

Your answer

Book answer

Quiz 19 score

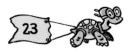

English QUIZ
20

Q6

Your answer Book answer

 1 The skin of an orange:
(a) **Peel** (b) **Pole** (c) **Pile** (d) **Pelt**

 2 Means the same as 'not difficult':
(a) **Simple** (b) **Sample** (c) **Example** (d) **Pimple**

 3 Shorten 'you will see' correctly:
(a) **You w'see** (b) **Yo' wi' see** (c) **You'll see** (d) **Youwl' see**

 4 Which of these is a noun?
(a) **Terrific** (b) **Tree** (c) **Tremble** (d) **Terrible**

 5 A word that rhymes with jolly:
(a) **Hilly** (b) **Pretty** (c) **Holly** (d) **Woolly**

Q4

 6 Who lived at Camelot?
(a) **Robin Hood** (b) **King Arthur** (c) **Gandalf** (d) **Noddy**

 7 Coins may … in your pocket:
(a) **Wrinkle** (b) **Clang** (c) **Jingle** (d) **Squeak**

 8 Find the noun here:
(a) **Pet** (b) **Lovely** (c) **Rainy** (d) **Terrible**

 9 Which of these is an adjective? Q8
(a) **Wind** (b) **Windy** (c) **Gale** (d) **Breeze**

 10 Which word rhymes with 'slow'?
(a) **Blue** (b) **Loud** (c) **Claw** (d) **Blow**

Quiz 20 score

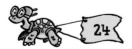

English QUIZ

21

Q5

 1 Which of these is not a verb?
(a) **Climb** (b) **Clean** (c) **Bend** (d) **Child**

Q1

 2 What you do in a pool?
(a) **Sing** (b) **Swing** (c) **Swim** (d) **Sleep**

 3 Opposite of correct:
(a) **Uncorrect** (b) **Incorrect** (c) **Imcorrect** (d) **Abcorrect**

 4 Can be a tool or fly in the air:
(a) **Plane** (b) **Train** (c) **Drain** (d) **Mane**

Q4

 5 Who had a coat of many colours?
(a) **Joseph** (b) **George** (c) **Henry** (d) **Daniel**

 6 Which bear has a friend named Bill Badger?
(a) **Teddy Robinson** (b) **Rupert** (c) **Paddington** (d) **Little Bear**

 7 A group of warships and a quick runner?
(a) **Fleet** (b) **Fast** (c) **Flotilla** (d) **Flurry**

 8 Which word could be a noun and a verb here?
(a) **Choose** (b) **Taste** (c) **Ask** (d) **Select**

 9 Which of these is a popular author?
(a) **Jiminy Cricket** (b) **A.J. Sprocket** (c) **Hyt Wicket** (d) **Lemony Snicket**

 10 Whose cat appears in a Christmas pantomime?
(a) **Robin Hood's** (b) **Dick Whittington's** (c) **Aladdin's** (d) **Mother Goose's**

Your answer

Book answer

Quiz 21 score

25

English QUIZ

22

Q2

 1 A covering for the face:
(a) **Mist**   (b) **Mask**   (c) **Musk**   (d) **Map**

 2 What kind of stories often have werewolves in them?
(a) **Horror**   (b) **Comic**   (c) **Historical**   (d) **Science fiction**

 3 Someone's life story is a … what?
(a) **Epic**   (b) **Novel**   (c) **Biography**   (d) **Nursery rhyme**

 4 Which is an exclamation mark?   Q10
(a) **%**   (b) **;**   (c) **!**   (d) **?**

 5 What a ship carries:
(a) **Carrot**   (b) **Carrion**   (c) **Cargo**   (d) **Caramel**

 6 An … is used to chop up wood?
(a) **Axe**   (b) **Axle**   (c) **Action**   (d) **Acrobat**

 7 Of which small band were Sleepy and Doc members?
(a) **Argonauts**   (b) **Famous Five**   (c) **Seven Dwarfs**   (d) **Robin Hood's outlaws**

 8 Spell the things you wear:
(a) **Jeans**   (b) **Genes**   (c) **Greens**   (d) **Jean's**   Q1

 9 What does the following punctuation mark mean – ;?
(a) **Semi-colon**   (b) **Apostrophe**   (c) **Comma**   (d) **Full stop**

 10 I'm very thirsty, I'd like a … what?
(a) **Sleep**   (b) **Walk**   (c) **Scratch**   (d) **Drink**

Quiz 22 score

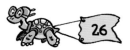

English QUIZ

23

Q3

 1 Is a gargantuan monster…?
(a) **Smelly** (b) **Green** (c) **Enormous** (d) **Tiny**

 2 Which abbreviation means 'turn over the page'?
(a) **VSO** (b) **DS0** (c) **BO** (d) **PTO**

 3 Complete the Rudyard Kipling title: *How the Elephant Got His* …?
(a) **Tail** (b) **Tusks** (c) **Trunk** (d) **Skin**

 4 A ruler in a kingdom:
(a) **King** (b) **Chief** (c) **Baron** (d) **Emperor**

Q7

 5 Many hands make light … what?
(a) **Work** (b) **Washing** (c) **Digging** (d) **Cooking**

 6 Spell the country in northern Europe:
(a) **Sweetden** (b) **Sueden** (c) **Swedun** (d) **Sweden**

 7 Which mythical bird came back to life from fire ashes?
(a) **Roc** (b) **Moa** (c) **Raven** (d) **Phoenix**

 8 Used to skim over snow:
(a) **Edge** (b) **Hedge** (c) **Sledge** (d) **Wedge**

 9 Which adjective best describes a shiny painted surface?
(a) **Graceful** (b) **Glowing** (c) **Grouchy** (d) **Glossy**

Q10

 10 A peal of what …?
(a) **Balls** (b) **Bells** (c) **Boxes** (d) **Birds**

Quiz 23 score

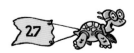

English QUIZ

24

Q5

Your answer | Book answer

1 Fill in the missing word: Jason picked up … shoes.
(a) **Her** (b) **His** (c) **Its** (d) **Their**

Q2

2 Another word for a sand bank:
(a) **Dune** (b) **Dun** (c) **Den** (d) **Dent**

3 What did Jack climb to meet a giant?
(a) **Ladder** (b) **Beanstalk** (c) **Mountain** (d) **Tree**

4 Another word for 'imitate':
(a) **Make** (b) **Copy** (c) **Play** (d) **Look**

5 In which Dickens' novel does the Artful Dodger appear?
(a) **A Christmas Carol** (b) **Oliver Twist** (c) **Great Expectations** (d) **Bleak House**

6 Who was the animal hero of the Uncle Remus stories?
(a) **Brer Rabbit** (b) **Moby Dick** (c) **Tarka the Otter** (d) **White Fang**

7 Could mean a yellow card in soccer:
(a) **Fowl** (b) **Foul** (c) **File** (d) **Foal**

8 What kind of animal is Anansi, hero of African folktales?
(a) **Snake** (b) **Leopard** (c) **Crocodile** (d) **Spider**

9 Spell the word that means 'scary':
(a) **Friytening** (b) **Frightening** (c) **Fritning** (d) **Fritening**

Q10

10 If something is worm-like, it could be:
(a) **Wriggly** (b) **Giggly** (c) **Ticklish** (d) **Fiddly**

Quiz 24 score

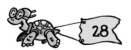
28

English QUIZ

25

Q3

		Your answer	Book answer

1. A stitch in time saves … what?
(a) **Money** (b) **Nine** (c) **Work** (d) **Eight**

2. Which word is something you cross on a country walk?
(a) **Mile** (b) **Pile** (c) **Stile** (d) **Tile**

3. Who wrote fables such as *The Hare and the Tortoise*?
(a) **Aesop** (b) **Aristotle** (c) **Alfred the Great** (d) **Alexander**

4. Which word rhymes with 'branch'?
(a) **Range** (b) **Ranch** (c) **Break** (d) **Lunch**

5. Which is a singular noun?   Q6
(a) **Feelings** (b) **Travels** (c) **Sky** (d) **Pictures**

6. What shape does Sirius Black adopt in the Harry Potter books?
(a) **Cow** (b) **Dragon** (c) **Snake** (d) **Dog**

7. A baby or very young child:
(a) **Infant** (b) **Veteran** (c) **Adolescent** (d) **Adult**

8. What was nasty about Medusa's hair?   Q10
(a) **Snaky** (b) **Smelly** (c) **Spiky** (d) **Slimy**

9. What word means the opposite of cautious?
(a) **Anxious** (b) **Impetuous** (c) **Slow** (d) **Frantic**

10. Which of these is not a noun?
(a) **Tom** (b) **Sophie** (c) **Cat** (d) **Slept**

Quiz 25 score

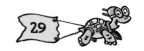

English QUIZ

26

Q3

| | Your answer | Book answer |

1 What would you not have 'a pair of'?
(a) **Jeans** (b) **Pyjamas** (c) **Scissors** (d) **Dinner**

2 Where should the apostrophe go, to shorten 'do not'?
(a) **Do'nt** (b) **D'ont** (c) **Dont'** (d) **Don't**

Q1

3 Who wrote *Little House on the Prairie*?
(a) **Beatrix Potter** (b) **Anna Sewell** (c) **Laura Ingalls Wilder** (d) **Pat Hutchins**

4 Something that can't be seen:
(a) **Impossible** (b) **Unnatural** (c) **Uncommon** (d) **Invisible**

5 Not clean:
(a) **Dark** (b) **Gloomy** (c) **Awful** (d) **Dirty**

6 What is the plural of goose?
(a) **Geese** (b) **Gosling** (c) **Gooses** (d) **Geeses**

Q5

7 Jules Verne's book, *Around the World in 80 …* what?
(a) **Seconds** (b) **Minutes** (c) **Days** (d) **Years**

8 Where a horse is kept:
(a) **Gable** (b) **Table** (c) **Fable** (d) **Stable**

9 Who told the story of the Wooden Horse of Troy?
(a) **Plato** (b) **Homer** (c) **Chaucer** (d) **Dickens**

10 A word that might describe a winter's day:
(a) **Silly** (b) **Chilly** (c) **Smelly** (d) **Sweaty**

Quiz 26 score

English QUIZ

27

Q8

| | Your answer | Book answer |

1 In which pantomime does Buttons appear?
(a) **Puss in Boots** (b) **Cinderella** (c) **Snow White** (d) **Robinson Crusoe**

2 The comparative of steep *(adjective)*:
(a) **Steep** (b) **Steeper** (c) **Steepey** (d) **Steepest**

3 The parent of a foal:
(a) **Cow** (b) **Horse** (c) **Pig** (d) **Sheep**

Q3

4 Which word means the time of year when leaves fall?
(a) **Autumn** (b) **Spring** (c) **Monsoon** (d) **January**

5 Which of these is another word for 'angry'?
(a) **Fast** (b) **Frightened** (c) **Fit** (d) **Furious**

6 Which is correct here?
(a) **Ten aples** (b) **Ten apples** (c) **Ten apple's** (d) **Ten appleses**

7 Complete the book title: *The Lion, the Witch and the* … what?
(a) **Wizard** (b) **Three Children** (c) **Wardrobe** (d) **Magic Chair**

8 As … as a bug in a rug?
(a) **Dead** (b) **Snug** (c) **Happy** (d) **Cosy**

Q7

9 To be immortal means … what?
(a) **To live for ever** (b) **To be a giant** (c) **To be an alien** (d) **To be famous**

10 Which word sounds the same as boot?
(a) **Loot** (b) **Soot** (c) **Short** (c) **Fat**

Quiz 27 score

31

English QUIZ

28

Q8

 1 What kind of animal was Jeremy Fisher?
(a) **Rabbit** (b) **Pig** (c) **Squirrel** (d) **Frog**

 2 Shorten 'I would like' using an apostrophe correctly:
(a) **I'd like** (b) **I wo'd like** (c) **I'd' like** (d) **'Id like**

 3 Logs sometimes do this on a fire:
(a) **Crackle** (b) **Cackle** (c) **Bustle** (d) **Jingle**

Q1

 4 The most famous Tank Engine is:
(a) **Timmy** (b) **Thomas** (c) **Charlie** (d) **Rupert**

 5 Spell the word that means the place where laws are made:
(a) **Parlymeant** (b) **Parleement** (c) **Parliament** (d) **Parleymint**

 6 What we wear to straighten our teeth:
(a) **Laces** (b) **Braces** (c) **Paces** (d) **Faces**

Q10

 7 Which of these is a plural noun?
(a) **Air** (b) **Sun** (c) **Clothes** (d) **Bath**

 8 The Minotaur was half human, half what?
(a) **Snake** (b) **Fish** (c) **Bull** (d) **Horse**

 9 Who was helped by Dr Watson?
(a) **Poirot** (b) **James Bond** (c) **Sherlock Holmes** (d) **Dr Doolittle**

 **10** Something you wear on your feet:
(a) **Kipper** (b) **Nipper** (c) **Slipper** (d) **Gripper**

Quiz 28 score

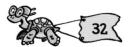

Chart Your Scores

English	1	2	3	4	5	6	7	8	9	10
Quiz 1										
Quiz 2										
Quiz 3										
Quiz 4										
Quiz 5										
Quiz 6										
Quiz 7										
Quiz 8										
Quiz 9										
Quiz 10										
Quiz 11										
Quiz 12										
Quiz 13										
Quiz 14										
Quiz 15										
Quiz 16										
Quiz 17										
Quiz 18										
Quiz 19										
Quiz 20										
Quiz 21										
Quiz 22										
Quiz 23										
Quiz 24										
Quiz 25										
Quiz 26										
Quiz 27										
Quiz 28										

HOMEWORK BUSTERS

Maths

Key to subject icons

 Measurement

 Number facts

 Shapes and angles

 Maths puzzles

 Working with numbers

 Calendars and time

Maths QUIZ

1

Your answer　**Book answer**

 1　What year will come 5 years after 2004?
(a) **2009**　(b) **2008**　(c) **2019**　(d) **2010**

 2　88 – 32 =?
(a) **50**　(b) **144**　(c) **46**　(d) **56**

Q7

 3　How many days are there in two weeks?
(a) **14**　(b) **20**　(c) **17**　(d) **30**

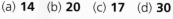

 4　What is 7 less than 84?
(a) **70**　(b) **72**　(c) **77**　(d) **79**

 5　What is the next number in the sequence 850, 800, 750, …?
(a) **700**　(b) **725**　(c) **900**　(d) **650**

 6　How many players in a soccer team (without subs)?
(a) **6**　(b) **11**　(c) **15**　(d) **22**

 7　How many quarters are there in a circle?
(a) **Two**　(b) **Four**　(c) **Six**　(d) **Eight**

Q9

 8　How many more is 41 than 27?
(a) **14**　(b) **10**　(c) **17**　(d) **23**

 9　What time is it 15 minutes after 3.40 p.m.?
(a) **3.15**　(b) **4.00**　(c) **5.10**　(d) **3.55**

 10　How many faces has a cylinder?
(a) **3**　(b) **2**　(c) **1**　(d) **6**

Quiz 1 score

Maths QUIZ

2

Q1

	Your answer	Book answer

 1 What shape is a wedge?
(a) **Cuboid** (b) **Triangle** (c) **Oval** (d) **Sphere**

 2 How many is three dozen?
(a) **30** (b) **36** (c) **35** (d) **300**

 3 How many degrees in a triangle?
(a) **160** (b) **200** (c) **180** (d) **360**

Q5

 4 What is a quarter of 24?
(a) **12** (b) **8** (c) **48** (d) **6**

 5 How many sides has a triangle?
(a) **Two** (b) **Three** (c) **Five** (d) **Six**

 6 What is 368,357 as a round number?
(a) **368,000** (b) **369,000** (c) **400,000** (d) **300,000**

 7 What time is 30 minutes after 3.40 p.m.?
(a) **3.55** (b) **4.10** (c) **4.20** (d) **4.25**

 8 Which number comes next: 2, 5, 11, 23, …?
(a) **24** (b) **47** (c) **46** (d) **100**

Q9

 9 If three teddies cost £9.60, how much is one teddy?
(a) **£3.20** (b) **£2.00** (c) **£4.00** (d) **£5.30**

 10 What time is 9 p.m. on a 24-hour clock?
(a) **09.00** (b) **90.00** (c) **21.00** (d) **29.00**

Quiz 2 score

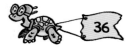 36

Maths QUIZ

3

Q2

Q5

		Your answer	Book answer

 1 What is 18 more than 31?
(a) **39** (b) **36** (c) **49** (d) **50**

 2 50% of a class of 30 are boys; how many are girls?
(a) **20** (b) **5** (c) **10** (d) **15**

 3 What is 23 less than 75?
(a) **52** (b) **25** (c) **50** (d) **98**

 4 How many centimetres are there in a metre?
(a) **5** (b) **10** (c) **50** (d) **100**

 5 How long is a journey that starts at 11.30 a.m. and ends at 12.25 p.m.?
(a) **35 minutes** (b) **55 minutes** (c) **25 minutes** (d) **1 hour**

 6 If you see four 5-spotted ladybirds, how many spots are there?
(a) **10** (b) **18** (c) **20** (d) **50**

Q6

 7 Which decimal measure is bigger than $1\frac{1}{4}$?
(a) **1.10** (b) **1.20** (c) **1.30** (d) **1.22**

 8 How many is a dozen?
(a) **12** (b) **13** (c) **20** (d) **144**

 9 If the 5.30 p.m. train leaves 5 minutes early, what time does it leave?
(a) **5.00** (b) **5.25** (c) **5.30** (d) **5.15**

 10 How many 3s are there in 42?
(a) **5** (b) **10** (c) **14** (d) **17**

Quiz 3 score

Maths QUIZ

4

Q1

| | | Your answer | Book answer |

 1 How many arms has an octopus?
(a) **2** (b) **4** (c) **6** (d) **8**

Q10

 2 How many degrees are there in a right angle?
(a) **90** (b) **45** (c) **180** (d) **360**

 3 How many runs does a cricketer score in a century?
(a) **10** (b) **50** (c) **100** (d) **150**

 4 What is 100 x 10?
(a) **110** (b) **150** (c) **1000** (d) **10,000**

 5 How many cards are there in a pack of playing cards?
(a) **52** (b) **12** (c) **13** (d) **100**

 6 What is the highest number (in spots) on one domino?
(a) **6** (b) **10** (c) **12** (d) **20**

Q5

 7 What year will come 5 years after 2004?
(a) **2009** (b) **2008** (c) **2019** (d) **2010**

 8 Which of these does not belong in this set?
(a) **2 x 3** (b) **4 + 2** (c) **1 + 5** (d) **15 – 10**

 9 Which is the sixth month of the year?
(a) **June** (b) **May** (c) **August** (d) **July**

 10 How many sides does a snow crystal have?
(a) **4** (b) **5** (c) **8** (d) **6**

Quiz 4 score

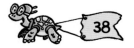

Maths QUIZ

5

Q8

		Your answer	Book answer
1	What is the area of a rectangle 10 x 15 cm? (a) **25 sq cm** (b) **150 sq cm** (c) **100 sq cm** (d) **1500 sq cm**	○	○
2	Which month always has the fewest number of days? (a) **February** (b) **December** (c) **May** (d) **January**	○	○
3	Which shape is a helix? (a) **Sphere** (b) **Spiral** (c) **Irregular hexagon** (d) **Cylinder**	○	○
4	How many sides has a dice? (a) **Two** (b) **Four** (c) **Six** (d) **Twelve**	○	○
5	How many letters in the alphabet? (a) **16** (b) **20** (c) **26** (d) **88**	○	○
6	What's the highest throw with two die (dice)? (a) **11** (b) **12** (c) **10** (d) **20**	○	○
7	'A bird in the hand'... is worth how many in the bush? (a) **None** (b) **One** (c) **Two** (d) **Ten**	○	○
8	What shape could you eat ice cream from? (a) **Cube** (b) **Cone** (c) **Triangle** (d) **Sphere**	○	○
9	How many days has September? (a) **28** (b) **29** (c) **30** (d) **31**	○	○
10	What is the square root of 16? (a) **8** (b) **10** (c) **4** (d) **32**	○	○

Q6

Q7

Quiz 5 score ▢

Maths QUIZ

6

Q1

 1 How many heads are better than one?
(a) **Two**   (b) **Three**   (c) **Four**   (d) **Ten**

 2 Which of these is an odd number: 2, 3, 4, 6?
(a) **2**   (b) **3**   (c) **4**   (d) **6**

 3 Round up 318 to the nearest ten.
(a) **310**   (b) **320**   (c) **330**   (d) **350**

 4 What is the square root of 100?
(a) **10**   (b) **200**   (c) **1000**   (d) **150**

Q5

 5 Share 36 pears equally between 12 people.
(a) **1 each**   (b) **2 each**   (c) **3 each**   (d) **Four each**

 6 How many degrees are there in a circle?
(a) **90**   (b) **180**   (c) **360**   (d) **400**

 7 How would you write one million?
(a) **100,000**   (b) **1,000,000**   (c) **10,000,000**   (d) **100,000,000**

 8 How many leaves has a 'lucky' clover?
(a) **Four**   (b) **Two**   (c) **Three**   (d) **Five**

Q8

 9 If 3 toys cost 50p each, how much change do you get from £5?
(a) **£1.00**   (b) **£2.25**   (c) **£3.50**   (d) **£3.00**

 10 If the temperature rises 7 degrees above 23°C, how warm is it?
(a) **24C°**   (b) **30°C**   (c) **28°C**   (d) **33°C**

Quiz 6 score

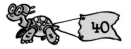

Maths QUIZ

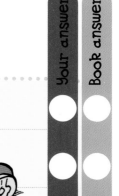

7

Q1

 1 If someone has quadruplets, how many babies are born?
(a) **Two**   (b) **Three**   (c) **Five**   (d) **Four**

 2 Which of these is a prime number?
(a) **2**   (b) **4**   (c) **6**   (d) **8**

 3 Pints, gallons and litres are all measurements of what?
(a) **Capacity**   (b) **length**   (c) **weight**   (d) **temperature**

 4 What shape is a shoe box?
(a) **Cuboid**   (b) **rectangle**   (c) **prism**   (d) **sphere**

Q4

 5 What is 10^2 (10 x 10)?
(a) **100**   (b) **20**   (c) **1000**   (d) **200**

 6 How many sides has a rectangle?
(a) **2**   (b) **4**   (c) **5**   (d) **10**

 7 What does mm stand for?
(a) **Millimetres**   (b) **Metres**   (c) **Miles**   (d) **Minutes**

 8 Counting in decimals means you:
(a) **Count in 10s**   (b) **Count in 2s**   (c) **Count in Is and 0s**   (d) **Count in 5s**

 9 In Roman numerals, what did C stand for?
(a) **10**   (b) **100**   (c) **1000**   (d) **10,000**

Q9

 10 How much change from £2.40 for three 60p-pens?
(a) **40p**   (b) **60p**   (c) **80p**   (d) **90p**

Quiz 7 score

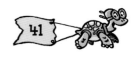

Maths QUIZ

8

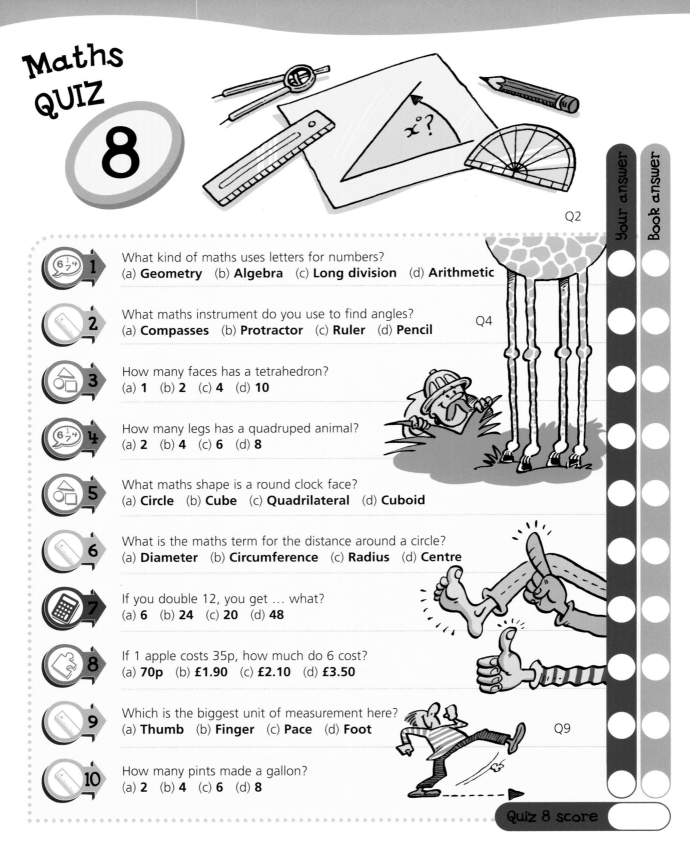

	Your answer	Book answer

1 What kind of maths uses letters for numbers?
(a) **Geometry** (b) **Algebra** (c) **Long division** (d) **Arithmetic**

2 What maths instrument do you use to find angles?
(a) **Compasses** (b) **Protractor** (c) **Ruler** (d) **Pencil**

3 How many faces has a tetrahedron?
(a) **1** (b) **2** (c) **4** (d) **10**

4 How many legs has a quadruped animal?
(a) **2** (b) **4** (c) **6** (d) **8**

5 What maths shape is a round clock face?
(a) **Circle** (b) **Cube** (c) **Quadrilateral** (d) **Cuboid**

6 What is the maths term for the distance around a circle?
(a) **Diameter** (b) **Circumference** (c) **Radius** (d) **Centre**

7 If you double 12, you get … what?
(a) **6** (b) **24** (c) **20** (d) **48**

8 If 1 apple costs 35p, how much do 6 cost?
(a) **70p** (b) **£1.90** (c) **£2.10** (d) **£3.50**

9 Which is the biggest unit of measurement here?
(a) **Thumb** (b) **Finger** (c) **Pace** (d) **Foot**

10 How many pints made a gallon?
(a) **2** (b) **4** (c) **6** (d) **8**

Q2

Q4

Q9

Quiz 8 score

Maths QUIZ

9

Q5

 1 What is the correct abbreviation for kilometre?
(a) **K**   (b) **km**   (c) **kilo**   (d) **kl**

 2 What is half of 96?
(a) **24**   (b) **43**   (c) **48**   (d) **50**

Q3

 3 If a book has 48 pages, which are the middle pages?
(a) **24 – 25**   (b) **20 – 21**   (c) **17 – 17**   (d) **32 – 33**

 4 How many feet make a yard?
(a) **One**   (b) **Two**   (c) **Three**   (d) **Six**

 5 What is the date of Christmas Day?
(a) **23 December**   (b) **25 December**   (c) **31 December**   (d) **1 January**

 6 If y = 3, how much is 3y?
(a) **0**   (b) **3**   (c) **6**   (d) **9**

 7 Which 3-coin set is worth £1.20?
(a) **50 + 50 + 20**   (b) **20 + 20 + 20**   (c) **50 + 20 + 10**   (d) **50 + 50 + 10**

 8 What shape is a dice?
(a) **Circle**   (b) **Irregular**   (c) **Cube**   (d) **Disc**

 9 Which set is biggest?
(a) **100 + 70 + 13**   (b) **30 + 73 + 56**   (c) **14 + 29 + 90**   (d) **50 + 17 + 23**

10 We ate 60% of a bunch of 50 grapes; how many did we eat?   Q10
(a) **10**   (b) **15**   (c) **30**   (d) **40**

Quiz 9 score

43

Maths QUIZ

10

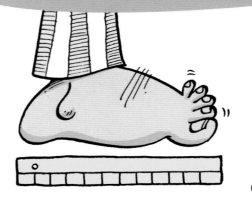

Q1

Your answer   **Book answer**

 1 How many inches make a foot?
(a) **2**   (b) **4**   (c) **10**   (d) **12**

 2 How many Sundays are there in four weeks?
(a) **1**   (b) **2**   (c) **3**   (d) **4**

 3 Add 1.3 to 4.8.
(a) **5.0**   (b) **4.9**   (c) **6.1**   (d) **7.3**

Q8

 4 What comes next on this number line: 28, 29, 30, 31, …?
(a) **26**   (b) **32**   (c) **27**   (d) **40**

 5 What is 17.50 hours on a 12-hour clock?
(a) **7.50 a.m.**   (b) **5.50 p.m.**   (c) **5.30 a.m.**   (d) **9.50 p.m.**

 6 What shape is a snooker ball?
(a) **Sphere**   (b) **Circle**   (c) **Square**   (d) **Rectangle**

 7 Subtract 15 from 85.
(a) **80**   (b) **70**   (c) **60**   (d) **65**

Q6

 8 What is the area of a rectangle 5 m x 3 m?
(a) **8 sq m**   (b) **10 sq m**   (c) **53 sq m**   (d) **15 sq m**

 9 If x + 20 = 29, what is x?
(a) **10**   (b) **20**   (c) **9**   (d) **49**

 10 6 + 3 − 4 is the same as which of these sums?
(a) **4 + 1**   (b) **2 + 2**   (c) **7 − 4**   (d) **8 − 6**

Quiz 10 score

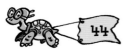 44

Maths QUIZ

11

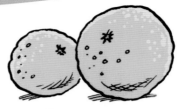

Q1

 1   How many halves in 3 wholes?
(a) **2**   (b) **3**   (c) **6**   (d) **9**

 2   Subtract 50 from 110.
(a) **60**   (b) **50**   (c) **70**   (d) **30**

 3   Find the next number in the sequence: 15, 30, 45, 60, …?
(a) **65**   (b) **75**   (c) **80**   (d) **85**

 4   What is x in this sum: $x - 4 = 16$?
(a) **12**   (b) **20**   (c) **18**   (d) **24**

Q5

 5   How many legs have six ants?
(a) **12**   (b) **36**   (c) **40**   (d) **48**

 6   How many odd numbers come before 12?
(a) **None**   (b) **3**   (c) **6**   (d) **11**

 7   What is 500 x 3?
(a) **1500**   (b) **150**   (c) **5000**   (d) **3500**

 8   How many 100s in 3000?
(a) **30**   (b) **10**   (c) **3**   (d) **300**

 9   Clare is 5 years older than Tom. If Tom is 8, how old is Clare?
(a) **3**   (b) **10**   (c) **13**   (d) **12**

 10   Find the answer to this chain sum: $2 + 3 + 5 - 3 = ?$
(a) **7**   (b) **14**   (c) **22**   (d) **3**

Q9

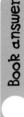

Quiz 11 score

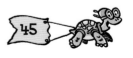

Maths QUIZ

12

Your answer | **Book answer**

1 Use two numbers and the – sign to make 19.
(a) **88 – 69** (b) **31 – 10** (c) **45 – 30** (d) **122 – 20**

2 Which of these numbers is nearest to 137?
(a) **130** (b) **135** (c) **140** (d) **147**

3 40% of 30 children have a pet; how many have pets?
(a) **4** (b) **8** (c) **12** (d) **14**

4 What time on a 24-hour clock is 15 minutes before midnight?
(a) **12.45** (b) **23.00** (c) **23.45** (d) **11.45**

5 How many toes are there on 6 feet?
(a) **20** (b) **30** (c) **10** (d) **35**

6 What is 2 x 4 x 2?
(a) **16** (b) **6** (c) **8** (d) **24**

Q5

7 How many 7s are there in 84?
(a) **10** (b) **12** (c) **14** (d) **18**

8 How many make a gross?
(a) **50** (b) **66** (c) **100** (d) **144**

9 Class 1 has 33 children, Class 2 has 29 children. How many altogether?
(a) **59** (b) **62** (c) **65** (d) **60**

10 What is a third of 36?
(a) **10** (b) **18** (c) **12** (d) **33**

Quiz 12 score

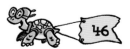

Maths QUIZ

13

Q1

| | Your answer | Book answer |

1 How long is a decade?
(a) **1 year** (b) **10 years** (c) **100 years** (d) **1000 years**

2 Use two numbers and the + sign to make 137.
(a) **60 + 77** (b) **100 + 57** (c) **90 + 27** (d) **80 + 67**

3 What is 4^3?
(a) **8** (b) **7** (c) **12** (d) **64**

Q4

4 How many times 9 is 99?
(a) **9** (b) **10** (c) **11** (d) **12**

5 Which numbers complete the pattern: 2 + 9 = 11, 12 + 9 = 21, 22 + 9 = 31, …?
(a) **32 + 9 = 41** (b) **22 + 10 = 32** (c) **2 + 19 = 21** (d) **22 + 11 = 33**

6 Which number pairs make 15?
(a) **8:4** (b) **7:10** (c) **8:7** (d) **8:8**

7 How long is a line 15 cm longer than 36 cm?
(a) **29 cm** (b) **32 cm** (c) **51 cm** (d) **46 cm**

Q10

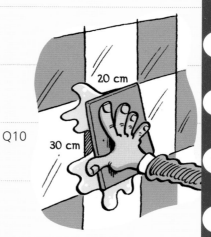

20 cm

30 cm

8 Add 24 to 31.
(a) **53** (b) **55** (c) **59** (d) **49**

9 What time is 15 minutes before ten past one?
(a) **12.55** (b) **1.25** (c) **1.00** (d) **12.45**

10 What is the area of a tile 20 cm x 10 cm?
(a) **100 sq cm** (b) **200 sq cm** (c) **210 sq cm** (d) **2000 sq cm**

Quiz 13 score

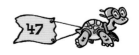

Maths QUIZ

14

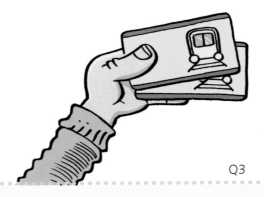

Q3

1 88 − 32 = ?
(a) **46** (b) **56** (c) **25** (d) **52**

2 Which of these pairs has a difference of 7?
(a) **19:12** (b) **8:2** (c) **15:6** (d) **20:10**

3 What is the cost of two train tickets at £15.60 each?
(a) **£24.80** (b) **£ 31.20** (c) **35.10** (d) **£40.00**

4 Which number comes next in this pattern: 5, 8, 11, 14?
(a) **15** (b) **17** (c) **19** (d) **22**

Q6

5 What is 30% of 150?
(a) **45** (b) **15** (c) **75** (d) **300**

6 How many legs have 15 dogs?
(a) **15** (b) **30** (c) **60** (d)**120**

7 Which fraction is the same as 0.25?
(a) **½** (b) **¼** (c) **²/₃** (d) **³/₄**

8 Which height is the tallest?
(a) **1.90 m** (b) **1.83 m** (c) **1.78 m** (d) **1.89 m**

9 What is half of 1½ hours?
(a) **20 minutes** (b) **45 minutes** (c) **35 minutes** (d) **60 minutes**

10 How many 50p coins make £5?
(a) **2** (b) **10** (c) **20** (d) **50**

Quiz 14 score

Maths QUIZ

15

1 How many trunks have 15 elephants?
(a) **30** (b) **15** (c) **60** (d) **100**

2 How many days are there in a leap year?
(a) **364** (b) **330** (c) **480** (d) **366**

3 Which pair has a difference of 27?
(a) **19:32** (b) **38:11** (c) **115:100** (d) **156:138**

4 Which month's name means '8th month'?
(a) **October** (b) **November** (c) **December** (d) **March**

5 Which of these pairs of playing cards do not add up to 16?
(a) **8 and 8** (b) **10 and 6** (c) **9 and 7** (d) **10 and 3**

6 What is 259 – 60?
(a) **253** (b) **200** (c) **199** (d) **158**

7 What is 321 ÷ 3?
(a) **100** (b) **99** (c) **107** (d) **318**

8 What angle is this?
(a) **90°** (b) **45°** (c) **180°** (d) **9°**

9 What shape is this?
(a) **Triangle** (b) **Square** (c) **Cube** (d) **Cylinder**

10 What is 15 less than 62?
(a) **50** (b) **47** (c) **57** (d) **39**

Your answer

Book answer

Quiz 15 score

49

Maths QUIZ

16

Q1

Your answer | Book answer

 1 Which of these is used in maths?
(a) **Pie chart**   (b) **Apple pie**   (c) **Pie crust**   (d) **Pie dish**

 2 Five ice creams cost £4; how much is one?
(a) **50p**   (b) **80p**   (c) **40p**   (d) **£1**

 3 If it's 10 minutes before noon, what time is it?
(a) **12.10 pm**   (b) **11.00 am**   (c) **11.50 am**   (d) **11.10 am**

Q3

4 Which of these coin sets = £ 2.50?
(a) **£1 + £1 + 50p**   (b) **50p + 50p + 50p**   (c) **£1 + 50p + 20p**   (d) **£1 + 50p + 50p**

 5 Which of these number pairs have a difference of 5?
(a) **2:6**   (b) **6:8**   (c) **6:11**   (d) **3:10**

 6 Which decimal measure is smaller than $2^3/_4$?
(a) **2.56**   (b) **2.48**   (c) **2.53**   (d) **2.75**

 7 How many 2s are there in 56?
(a) **10**   (b) **14**   (c) **50**   (d) **28**

Q2

 8 Take 2500 away from 5700.
(a) **3200**   (b) **570**   (c) **2500**   (d) **2200**

 9 What is 3^2?
(a) **5**   (b) **6**   (c) **9**   (d) **33**

 10 In which century was the year 1588?
(a) **13th**   (b) **15th**   (c) **18th**   (d) **16th**

Quiz 16 score

Maths QUIZ

17

Q3

 1 What is 10 + 9 multiplied by 2?
(a) **19**   (b) **38**   (c) **180**   (d) **21**

 2 How many 8s in 64?
(a) **4**   (b) **6**   (c) **8**   (d) **10**

 3 If one pig weigh 25 kg, how heavy are 5 pigs?
(a) **100 kg**   (b) **125 kg**   (c) **200 kg**   (c) **250 kg**

 4 How many 3s make 21?
(a) **7**   (b) **6**   (c) **5**   (d) **11**

 5 Which is biggest?
(a) **1000 x 5**   (b) **50 x 100**   (c) **10 x 5000**   (d) **100 x 10**

 6 Which of these is a kind of graph?
(a) **Pole**   (b) **Bar**   (c) **Rib**   (d) **Knuckle**

Q7

 7 What shape is a pencil?
(a) **Cone**   (b) **Square**   (c) **Prism**   (d) **Cylinder**

 8 How could you split a 16-slice pizza fairly between four people?
(a) **16 slices each**   (b) **5 slices each**   (c) **4 slices each**   (d) **2 slices each**

 9 How many legs have 11 giraffes?
(a) **44**   (b) **11**   (c) **22**   (d) **144**

Q8

 10 What is 7.30 am on a 24-hour clock?
(a) **15.30**   (b) **19.30**   (c) **77.30**   (d) **07.30**

Quiz 17 score

51

Maths
QUIZ
18

Q2

 1 What is the smallest quantity here?
(a) **0.50**   (b) **0.39**   (c) **0.072**   (d) **0.92**

 2 How would you find the volume of a box?
(a) **10 x Height**   (b) **Length x Width x Height**   (c) **Area ÷ 2**   (d) **Length x Width**

 3 In which century was the year 1815?
(a) **15th**   (b) **16th**   (c) **18th**   (d) **19th**

 4 Which date comes after 28th February (except in a leap year)?
(a) **1st March**   (b) **29th February**   (c) **30th February**   (d) **1st April**

 5 How many runs is a duck in cricket?   Q5
(a) **0**   (b) **10**   (c) **50**   (d) **100**

 6 How many 5s in 75?
(a) **3**   (b) **15**   (c) **20**   (d) **13**

 7 How much change from £10 for a meal costing £8.80?
(a) **£1.00**   (b) **£1.20**   (c) **£2.00**   (d) **£2.10**

 8 Which is the biggest fraction?
(a) $^3/_{18}$ (b) $^3/_8$ (c) $^3/_{16}$ (d) $^3/_{10}$

Q7

 9 If x = 2 and y = 5, what is x + y?
(a) **7**   (b) **3**   (c) **2**   (d) **10**

 10 Which set in biggest?
(a) **10 + 13 + 5**   (b) **10 + 10 + 10**   (c) **13 + 13 + 3**   (d) **1 + 13 + 14**

Quiz 18 score

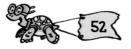

Maths QUIZ

19

Q5

Your answer

Book answer

 1 How long does a trip of 550 km take at average speed of 50 km per hour?
(a) **5 hours**   (b) **11 hours**   (c) **10 hours**   (d) **24 hours**

 2 Which is the next number: 3, 9, 27, …?
(a) **30**   (b) **54**   (c) **81**   (d) **100**

 3 What year came immediately before 1900?
(a) **1799**   (b) **1899**   (c) **1901**   (d) **1890**

Q6

 4 What is 77 – 59?
(a) **15**   (b) **16**   (c) **18**   (d) **20**

 5 How many colours has a tricolour flag?
(a) **One**   (b) **Two**   (c) **Three**   (d) **Five**

 6 How many 400-m laps do runners complete in a 1500 m race?
(a) **One**   (b) **Three**   (c) **Five**   (d) **Ten**

 7 How many sides are there in a pentagon?
(a) **3**   (b) **5**   (c) **7**   (d) **10**

Q8

 8 How many legs have a pair of twins?
(a) **4**   (b) **8**   (c) **2**   (d) **6**

 9 If two jars cost £3.50, how much is one jar?
(a) **£1.50**   (b) **£1.75**   (c) **£7.00**   (d) **£3.00**

 10 If a film starts at 2.30 p.m. and last 2.5 hours, what time does it end?
(a) **3 o'clock**   (b) **4 o'clock**   (c) **5 o' clock**   (d) **6 o'clock**

Quiz 19 score

53

Maths QUIZ

20

Q2

		Your answer	Book answer

1 Which of these fractions is the same as 0.5?
(a) ¾   (b) ½   (c) ¼   (d) ⅔

2 Which is the tallest of these people's heights?
(a) **1.91 m**   (b) **1.67 m**   (c) **1.83 m**   (d) **1.79 m**

3 What is half of 2½ hours?
(a) **75 minutes**   (b) **60 minutes**   (c) **1 hour**   (d) **3 hours**

Q5

4 Which is longest?
(a) **Yard**   (b) **Metre**   (c) **Centimetre**   (d) **Inch**

5 How many 50p coins make £10?
(a) **Two**   (b) **Five**   (c) **Ten**   (d) **Twenty**

6 How many hours in a week?
(a) **12**   (b) **24**   (c) **52**   (d) **168**

7 How many tens in a dozen?
(a) **None**   (b) **One**   (c) **Two**   (d) **Twenty**

Q10

8 How much is 50 + 14 + 3?
(a) **64**   (b) **57**   (c) **53**   (d) **67**

9 What is 5 in Roman numerals?
(a) **II**   (b) **V**   (c) **X**   (d) **C**

10 12 children share three boats: how many in each boat?
(a) **4**   (b) **6**   (b) **3** (c)   (d) **5**

Quiz 20 score

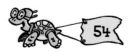
54

Maths QUIZ

21

Q2

 1 What are seven sevens?
(a) **14**   (b) **21**   (c) **49**   (d) **70**

 2 There are 5 glue sticks in one pack: how many in 6 packs?
(a) **30**   (b) **11**   (c) **15**   (d) **15**

 3 Which of these is an even number: 7, 10, 15, 21?
(a) **7**   (b) **10**   (c) **15**   (d) **21**

 4 What is 88 ÷ 11?
(a) **8**   (b) **10**   (c) **99**   (d) **77**

Q7

 5 How many 12s in 144?
(a) **10**   (b) **12**   (c) **20**   (d) **50**

 6 Multiply 5 x 3.
(a) **6**   (b) **8**   (c) **15**   (d) **21**

 7 What unit would you weigh a whale in?
(a) **Tonne**   (b) **Litre**   (c) **Gram**   (d) **Kilometre**

 8 What is one-third of 33?
(a) **3**   (b) **10**   (c) **11**   (d) **99**

 9 What is 5^2?
(a) **18**   (b) **27**   (c) **25**   (d) **90**

 10 How many Ancient Wonders of the World were there?
(a) **Two**   (b) **Seven**   (c) **Five**   (d) **Nine**

Q10

Quiz 21 score

Maths QUIZ

22

Q2

| | Your answer | Book answer |

1 A van travels 4 km on 1 litre of petrol. How far can it go on 8 litres?
(a) **2 km**   (b) **8 km**   (c) **12 km**   (d) **32 km**

2 If 10% of a class of 30 children are off ill, how many are unwell?
(a) **3**   (b) **5**   (c) **10**   (d) **13**

3 What number is one followed by three zeros?
(a) **Ten**   (b) **Hundred**   (c) **Thousand**   (d) **Million**

Q5

4 How much less than 120 is 80?
(a) **20**   (b) **100**   (c) **80**   (d) **40**

5 How can 18 oranges be divided equally among 9 children?
(a) **1 each**   (b) **2 each**   (c) **3 each**   (d) **4 each**

6 How many 2s in 36?
(a) **8**   (b) **10**   (c) **12**   (d) **18**

7 What did X in Roman numerals stand for?
(a) **1**   (b) **5**   (c) **10**   (d) **50**

8 What is measured in hectares?
(a) **Length**   (b) **Liquid**   (c) **Land area**   (d) **Haircuts**

9 Multiply 10 x 10 x 10
(a) **100**   (b) **1000**   (c) **10,000**   (d) **1,000,000**

Q7

10 Divide 96 by 12
(a) **84**   (b) **8**   (c) **10**   (d) **108**

Quiz 22 score

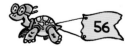

Maths QUIZ

23

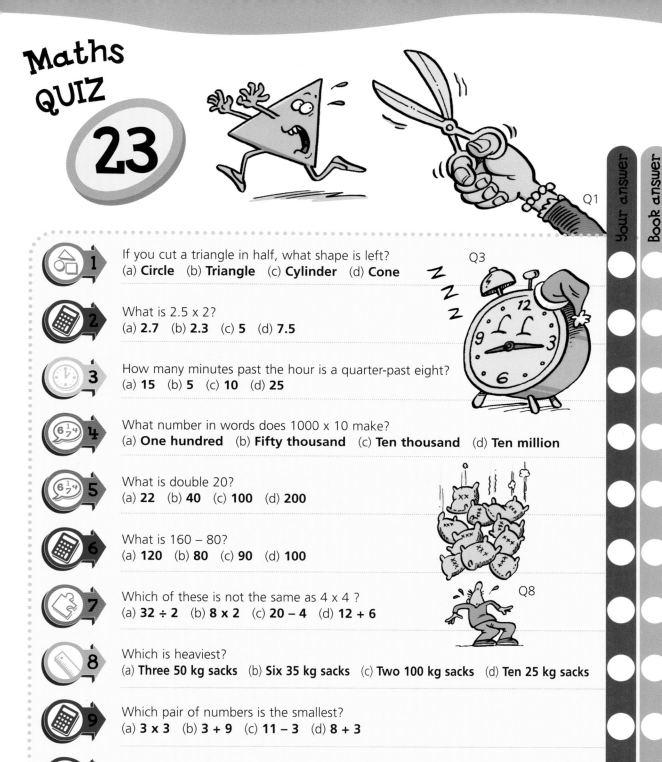

		Your answer	Book answer

1 If you cut a triangle in half, what shape is left?
(a) **Circle** (b) **Triangle** (c) **Cylinder** (d) **Cone**

2 What is 2.5 x 2?
(a) **2.7** (b) **2.3** (c) **5** (d) **7.5**

3 How many minutes past the hour is a quarter-past eight?
(a) **15** (b) **5** (c) **10** (d) **25**

4 What number in words does 1000 x 10 make?
(a) **One hundred** (b) **Fifty thousand** (c) **Ten thousand** (d) **Ten million**

5 What is double 20?
(a) **22** (b) **40** (c) **100** (d) **200**

6 What is 160 – 80?
(a) **120** (b) **80** (c) **90** (d) **100**

7 Which of these is not the same as 4 x 4 ?
(a) **32 ÷ 2** (b) **8 x 2** (c) **20 – 4** (d) **12 + 6**

8 Which is heaviest?
(a) **Three 50 kg sacks** (b) **Six 35 kg sacks** (c) **Two 100 kg sacks** (d) **Ten 25 kg sacks**

9 Which pair of numbers is the smallest?
(a) **3 x 3** (b) **3 + 9** (c) **11 – 3** (d) **8 + 3**

10 Which number is 15 more than 172?
(a) **87** (b) **167** (c) **200** (d) **187**

Quiz 23 score

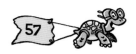

Maths QUIZ

24

Q9

1 Which is the odd number here?
(a) **222** (b) **333** (c) **444** (d) **666**

2 Which is the biggest set?
(a) **7 + 5 + 10** (b) **8 + 9 + 11** (c) **3 + 6 + 14** (d) **2 + 14 + 5**

3 Which unit measures length?
(a) **Square metre** (b) **Cubic Metre** (c) **Metre** (d) **Litre**

Q7

4 What is the correct maths name for 0?
(a) **Nothing** (b) **Nil** (c) **Nowt** (d) **Zero**

5 Which is the biggest?
(a) **10 x 75** (b) **11 x 80** (c) **9 x 100** (d) **10 x 89**

6 How many inches in a foot?
(a) **3** (b) **9** (c) **12** (d) **24**

7 How heavy are three 40 kg boxes?
(a) **120 kg** (b) **100 kg** (c) **12 kg** (d) **240 kg**

8 What shape is this?
(a) **Square** (b) **Cone** (c) **Cube** (d) **Triangle**

9 Which of these signs means 'divide by'?
(a) **%** (b) **÷** (c) **π** (d) **=**

Q8

10 Un, deux, trois is one, two, three in what language?
(a) **Latin** (b) **French** (c) **Spanish** (d) **German**

Quiz 24 score

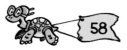
58

Maths QUIZ

25

Q3

| | Your answer | Book answer |

 1 Which of these is a degree sign?
(a) ° (b) ¿ (c) Ω (d) π

 2 What shape is the face of a cube?
(a) **Triangle** (b) **Square** (c) **Circle** (d) **Rhomboid**

 3 Roughly how big is a soccer field?
(a) **10 hectares** (b) **1 hectare** (c) **4000 litres** (d) **10 kilometres**

 4 If a carpet measures 5 m x 10 m, what is its area?
(a) **15 sq m** (b) **110 sq m** (c) **50 sq m** (d) **500 sq m**

 5 What is 8.30 am on a 24-hour clock?
(a) **08.30** (b) **16.30** (c) **80.30** (d) **20.30**

Q2

 6 Which number is missing from this sequence: 16, 15, ..., 13, 12 ?
(a) **11** (b) **14** (c) **17** (d) **20**

 7 How many miles is a marathon race?
(a) **5** (b) **15** (c) **26** (d) **100**

 8 Write 333 to the nearest 50.
(a) **350** (b) **330** (c) **300** (d) **300**

 9 How much do two apples cost, at 45p each?
(a) **90p** (b) **9p** (c) **80p** (d) **£1.10**

Q9

 10 How many 10ps are there in a pound?
(a) **10** (b) **20** (c) **15** (d) **30**

Quiz 25 score

59

Maths QUIZ

26

Q5

	Your answer	Book answer

 1 How many fives are there in 43 (with a remainder)?
(a) **3**   (b) **5**   (c) **8**   (d) **10**

 2 Which of these would you measure in grams?
(a) **Flour**   (b) **Mountains**   (c) **Wine**   (d) **Electricity**

 3 Which of these numbers is odd?
(a) **14**   (b) **44**   (c) **77**   (d) **120**

 4 What is 21 more than 14?
(a) **26**   (b) **35**   (c) **33**   (d) **45**

 5 How many planets orbit our Sun?
(a) **Five**   (b) **Nine**   (c) **Ten**   (d) **Fifty**

Q2

 6 What is the biggest number you can make from 2, 5 and 7?
(a) **527**   (b) **752**   (c) **257**   (d) **7500**

Q8

 7 What is half of 50?
(a) **5**   (b) **10**   (c) **25**   (d) **100**

 8 In what century was the year 1066?
(a) **8th**   (b) **9th**   (c) **10th**   (d) **11th**

 9 Multiply 6 x 8.
(a) **14**   (b) **32**   (c) **16**   (d) **48**

 10 What is the square root of 16?
(a) **4**   (b) **7**   (c) **2**   (d) **32**

Quiz 26 score

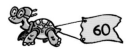

Maths QUIZ

27

Your answer **Book answer**

1. What shape is a soccer ball?
   (a) **Sphere** (b) **Cuboid** (c) **Square** (d) **Ellipse**

2. Add 124 and 53
   (a) **178** (b) **177** (c) **227** (d) **170**

3. What must be added to 22 to make 30?
   (a) **7** (b) **10** (c) **8** (d) **12**

4. What is 30% of 200?
   (a) **60** (b) **20** (c) **70** (d) **100**

5. How many right angles are there in a square?
   (a) **Four** (b) **Six** (c) **Eight** (d) **Ten**

Q5

6. In what units are apples weighed?
   (a) **Litres** (b) **Kilograms** (c) **Centimetres** (d) **Cores**

7. If x = 2, what is 10 x?
   (a) **12** (b) **20** (c) **200** (d) **8**

Q9

8. What shape is an ellipse?
   (a) **Oval** (b) **Round** (c) **Square** (d) **Cube**

9. What is the highest 3-dart score on a darts board?
   (a) **20** (b) **60** (c) **100** (d) **180**

10. Which is the smallest of these sets?
    (a) **150 – 70** (b) **20 x 5** (c) **200 – 100** (d) **500 ÷ 5**

Quiz 27 score

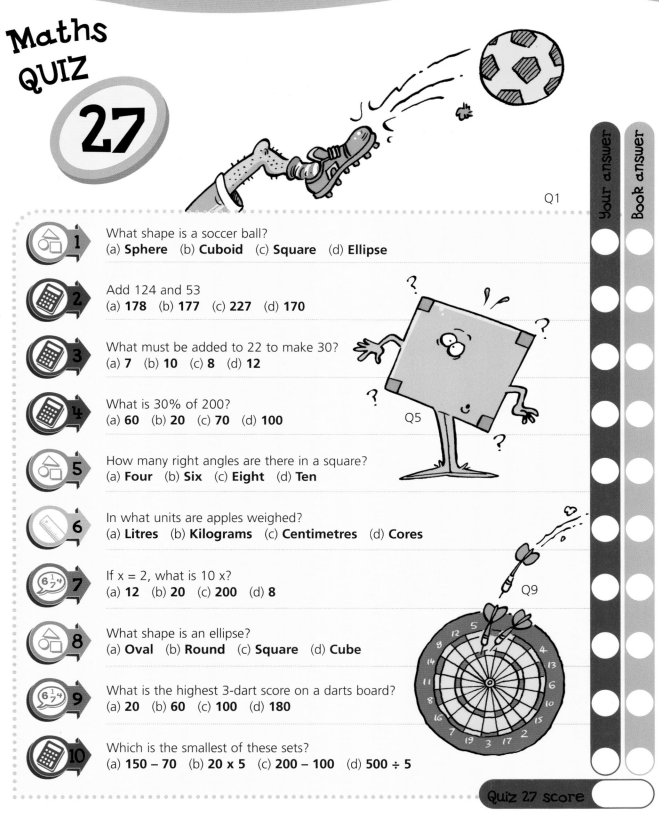

Maths QUIZ

28

	Your answer	Book answer

 1 x + 28 = 35. How much is x?
(a) **3**   (b) **5**   (c) **7**   (d) **10**

 2 15 children read 30 books in one week. What's the average weekly read?
(a) **1 book**   (b) **2 books**   (c) **3 books**   (d) **5 books**

 3 Which of these is said to be an 'unlucky number'?
(a) **2**   (b) **8**   (c) **13**   (d) **100**

Q3

 4 How many sixes are there in 72?
(a) **6**   (b) **10**   (c) **12**   (d) **15**

 5 Which is the closest estimate for the weight of an elephant?
(a) **60 grams**   (b) **6 kilograms**   (c) **6 tonnes**   (d) **60 tonnes**

 6 How many degrees are there in a circle?
(a) **180**   (b) **100**   (c) **1000**   (d) **360**

Q5

 7 Which is the smallest of these sets?
(a) **2 + 2 + 2**   (b) **3 x 3**   (c) **9 – 2**   (d) **7 + 1 + 0**

 8 How many players are there in a rugby union team?
(a) **15**   (b) **11**   (c) **22**   (d) **40**

 9 How old is 'three score years and ten'?
(a) **18**   (b) **50**   (c) **70**   (d) **100**

 10 What is the number of the Prime Minister's Downing Street home?
(a) **1**   (b) **10**   (c) **11**   (d) **20**

Quiz 28 score

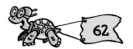

Chart Your Scores

Maths	1	2	3	4	5	6	7	8	9	10
Quiz 1										
Quiz 2										
Quiz 3										
Quiz 4										
Quiz 5										
Quiz 6										
Quiz 7										
Quiz 8										
Quiz 9										
Quiz 10										
Quiz 11										
Quiz 12										
Quiz 13										
Quiz 14										
Quiz 15										
Quiz 16										
Quiz 17										
Quiz 18										
Quiz 19										
Quiz 20										
Quiz 21										
Quiz 22										
Quiz 23										
Quiz 24										
Quiz 25										
Quiz 26										
Quiz 27										
Quiz 28										

Science

Key to subject icons

 Science and technology

 Scientists at work

 Earth

 Space

 Human body

 Inventions and machines

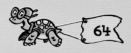

science QUIZ

1

Q3

 1 What do we call the water vapour that comes out of a kettle?
(a) **Steam** (b) **Mist** (c) **Dew** (d) **Hail**

 2 Which of these words means a vapour turning back to a liquid?
(a) **Evaporation** (b) **Compensation** (c) **Condensation** (d) **Dehydration**

 3 What do we call a twisting windstorm over land?
(a) **Waterspout** (b) **Monsoon** (c) **Blizzard** (d) **Tornado**

 4 What are all elements made of?
(a) **Molecules** (b) **Gases** (c) **Rocks** (d) **Bacteria**

Q5

 5 What rocky object circles the Earth?
(a) **The Shuttle** (b) **The Space Station** (c) **The Moon** (d) **Mars**

 6 What process can turn seawater into drinking water?
(a) **Distillation** (b) **Rusting** (c) **Burning** (d) **Freezing**

 7 What happens to glass when it is heated?
(a) **Turns black** (b) **Freezes** (c) **Softens** (d) **Vanishes**

8 Valentina Tereshkova was the first woman … what?
(a) **Glider pilot** (b) **Balloonist** (c) **Nobel prizewinner** (d) **Astronaut**

Q9

 9 What kind of machine was the 1908 Ford Model T?
(a) **Bicycle** (b) **Vacuum cleaner** (c) **Car** (d) **Television**

 10 What is limestone?
(a) **Drink** (b) **Rock** (c) **Acid** (d) **Spacedust**

Your answer

Book answer

Quiz 1 score

65

science QUIZ 2

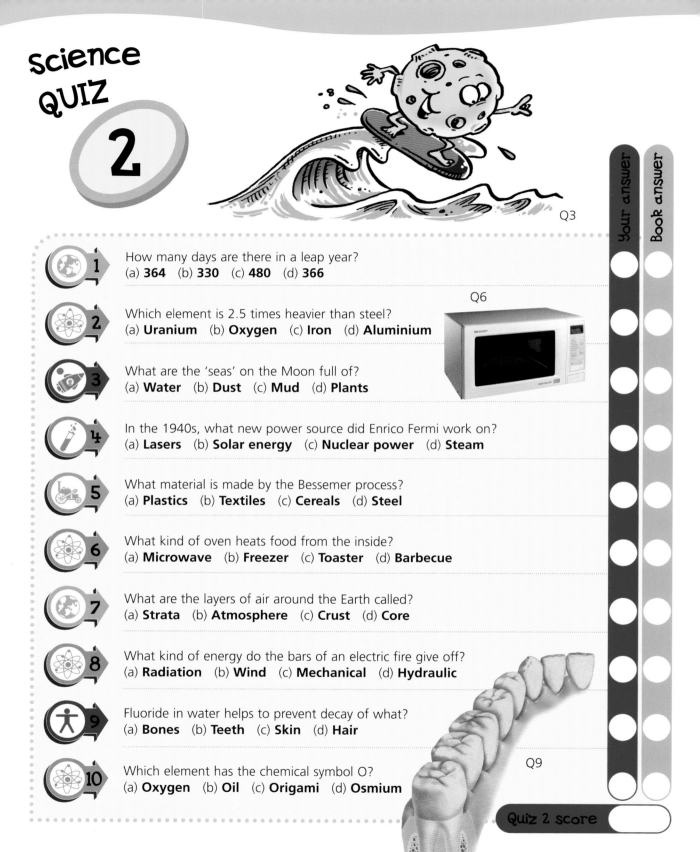

		Your answer	Book answer
1	How many days are there in a leap year? (a) **364** (b) **330** (c) **480** (d) **366**	○	○
2	Which element is 2.5 times heavier than steel? (a) **Uranium** (b) **Oxygen** (c) **Iron** (d) **Aluminium**	○	○
3	What are the 'seas' on the Moon full of? (a) **Water** (b) **Dust** (c) **Mud** (d) **Plants**	○	○
4	In the 1940s, what new power source did Enrico Fermi work on? (a) **Lasers** (b) **Solar energy** (c) **Nuclear power** (d) **Steam**	○	○
5	What material is made by the Bessemer process? (a) **Plastics** (b) **Textiles** (c) **Cereals** (d) **Steel**	○	○
6	What kind of oven heats food from the inside? (a) **Microwave** (b) **Freezer** (c) **Toaster** (d) **Barbecue**	○	○
7	What are the layers of air around the Earth called? (a) **Strata** (b) **Atmosphere** (c) **Crust** (d) **Core**	○	○
8	What kind of energy do the bars of an electric fire give off? (a) **Radiation** (b) **Wind** (c) **Mechanical** (d) **Hydraulic**	○	○
9	Fluoride in water helps to prevent decay of what? (a) **Bones** (b) **Teeth** (c) **Skin** (d) **Hair**	○	○
10	Which element has the chemical symbol O? (a) **Oxygen** (b) **Oil** (c) **Origami** (d) **Osmium**	○	○

Q3

Q6

Q9

Quiz 2 score ○

Science QUIZ

3

Q9

1 What is the common name for sodium chloride?
(a) **Salt**   (b) **Soap**   (c) **Sugar**   (d) **Vinegar**

Q1

2 Sulphuric, nitric and hydrochloric are all kinds of what?
(a) **Gas**   (b) **Mineral**   (c) **Base**   (d) **Acid**

3 Which plants are most affected by acid rain?
(a) **Trees**   (b) **Cacti**   (c) **Vegetables**   (d) **Seaweed**

4 Which body part does coronary disease affect?
(a) **Stomach**   (b) **Liver**   (c) **Kidneys**   (d) **Heart**

5 Which chemical family do plastics belong to?
(a) **Crystals**   (b) **Polymers**   (c) **Acids**   (d) **Salts**

6 What do we call the jagged points on the edge of a saw?
(a) **Fingers**   (b) **Teeth**   (c) **Claws**   (d) **Nails**

7 What were Monotype and Linotype machines used for?
(a) **Printing**   (b) **Floorlaying**   (c) **Cooking**   (d) **Teaching**

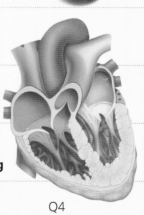

8 Rayon and nylon are examples of what?
(a) **Gases**   (b) **Metals**   (c) **Stars**   (d) **Synthetic textiles**

Q4

9 What do scientists measure on the Richter scale?
(a) **Caves**   (b) **Stars**   (c) **Earthquakes**   (d) **Bones**

10 Which part of a ship steers it?
(a) **Mast**   (b) **Propeller**   (c) **Keel**   (d) **Rudder**

Your answer   **Book answer**

Quiz 3 score

science QUIZ

4

Q9

Your answer | **Book answer**

1 What kind of machine has a hard drive?
(a) **Computer** (b) **Tractor** (c) **Bus** (d) **Tank**

2 What kind of material is PVC?
(a) **Wool** (b) **Plastic** (c) **Metal** (d) **Wood**

3 How many times a minute does an adult's heart beat?
(a) **100** (b) **70** (c) **50** (d) **200**

Q1

4 What are rocks made of?
(a) **Minerals** (b) **Plants** (c) **Gas** (d) **Ice**

5 What is a weaving machine called?
(a) **Plane** (b) **Loom** (c) **Grabbler** (d) **Lathe**

6 What kind of boat has two hulls?
(a) **Canoe** (b) **Catamaran** (c) **Barge** (d) **Clipper**

7 What is the name of our galaxy?
(a) **Dragon** (b) **Great Bear** (c) **Milky Way** (d) **Perseus**

8 What bones make the 'cage' in your chest?
(a) **Stirrups** (b) **Braces** (c) **Locks** (d) **Ribs**

Q10

9 What force drives a pneumatic drill?
(a) **Air** (b) **Water** (c) **Heat** (d) **Friction**

10 What is the smallest living unit?
(a) **Atom** (b) **Cell** (c) **Calorie** (d) **Gram**

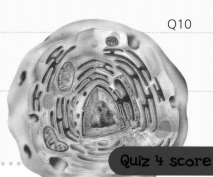

Quiz 4 score

science QUIZ 5

Q2

 1   If a lens curves inwards, what shape is it?
(a) **Cavernous**   (b) **Concave**   (c) **Convex**   (d) **Converted**

 2   What is the name of the bony case inside your head?
(a) **Hip**   (b) **Skull**   (c) **Kneecap**   (d) **Pelvis**

 3   What is another name for a space traveller?
(a) **Nomad**   (b) **Aquanaut**   (c) **Astronaut**   (d) **Navigator**

Q2

 4   What machine dives deepest into the ocean?
(a) **Diving bell**   (b) **U-boat**   (c) **Bathyscaphe**   (d) **Jetski**

 5   Which unit is used to measure electric current?
(a) **Amp**   (b) **Degree**   (c) **Kilogram**   (d) **Litre**

 6   What are cumulus and nimbus forms of?
(a) **Corals**   (b) **Rocks**   (c) **Clouds**   (d) **Stars**

 7   What do we call a mixture of two metals?
(a) **Muggle**   (b) **Blend**   (c) **Tincture**   (d) **Alloy**

Q4

 8   What is the name of the connection where two bones meet?
(a) **Junction**   (b) **Bracket**   (c) **Hinge**   (d) **Joint**

 9   What does a ship drop to stop it drifting?
(a) **Ballast**   (b) **Keel**   (c) **Anchor**   (d) **Mast**

 10   Who invented a raised-dot reading system for blind people?
(a) **Morse**   (b) **Braille**   (c) **Barnardo**   (d) **Baird**

Quiz 5 score

science QUIZ

6

	Your answer	Book answer

 1 How long does it take the Earth to orbit the Sun?
(a) **365 days** (b) **100 days** (c) **400 days** (d) **500 days**

Q2

 2 Which of these would you find in a laboratory?
(a) **Growbag** (b) **Test tube** (c) **Gavel** (d) **Trampoline**

 3 What do we call a drug that eases pain?
(a) **Cordial** (b) **Laxative** (c) **Anaesthetic** (d) **Catalyst**

 4 What is the positive (+) electrode in an electric circuit called?
(a) **Diode** (b) **Anode** (c) **North Pole** (d) **Electron**

 5 What kind of machine can lift a load, such as a car?
(a) **Jack** (b) **Screwdriver** (c) **Clamp** (d) **Press**

 6 What do we call a very hot oven used for melting metals?
(a) **Bath** (b) **Fume chamber** (c) **Furnace** (d) **Compost heap**

 7 What makes things far away look bigger?
(a) **Telepathy** (b) **Telephone** (c) **Television** (d) **Telescope**

 8 Which part of the body might be helped by a pacemaker?
(a) **Feet** (b) **Heart** (c) **Ears** (d) **Spine**

 9 What is the name of the point at which a lever tilts?
(a) **Focal point** (b) **Axle** (c) **Spoke** (d) **Fulcrum**

Q10

 10 To which planet was the *Sojourner* robot sent?
(a) **Venus** (b) **Jupiter** (c) **Saturn** (d) **Mars**

Quiz 6 score

science QUIZ

7

Q7

 1 What do we call the use of radio waves to detect objects?
(a) **Robotics**   (b) **Radar**   (c) **VHF**   (d) **Enigma**

 2 What kind of engine does a Boeing 747 airliner have?
(a) **Turboprop**   (b) **Steam**   (c) **Diesel**   (d) **Turbofan**

 3 In 1957 what was the first animal to fly in space?
(a) **Dog**   (b) **Cat**   (c) **Monkey**   (d) **Fish**

Q3

 4 Which of these units measures power?
(a) **Degree**   (b) **Litre**   (c) **Watt** (c)   (d) **Centimetre**

 5 What are molars?
(a) **Toes**   (b) **Teeth**   (c) **Bones**   (d) **Enzymes**

 6 What fuel is made by heating coal?
(a) **Coke**   (b) **Natural gas**   (c) **Paraffin**   (d) **Wax**

 7 For what invention is James Watt famous?
(a) **Steam engine**   (b) **Bicycle**   (c) **Gunpowder**   (d) **Television**

 8 How much bigger than the Moon is the Earth?
(a) **4 times**   (b) **10 times**   (c) **100 times**   (d) **400 times**

 9 Which rays take pictures of the inside of your body?
(a) **Infrared**   (b) **Ultraviolet**   (c) **Gamma**   (d) **X-rays**   Q9

 10 What do we call a fastener with two rows of teeth?
(a) **Button**   (b) **Popper**   (c) **Zip/Zipper**   (d) **Bolt**

Quiz 7 score

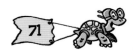

science QUIZ

8

Q4

Your answer   Book answer

1 What is the name of the shaft on which a wheel turns?
(a) **Rim**   (b) **Axle**   (c) **Hub**   (d) **Spoke**

2 Which vitamin is found in oranges and lemons?
(a) **Vitamin A**   (b) **Vitamin B**   (c) **Vitamin C**   (d) **Vitamin D**

3 Which simple machine shows you where magnetic north is?
(a) **Astrolabe**   (b) **Sextant**   (c) **Solenoid**   (d) **Compass**

Q3

4 What do we measure in decibels?
(a) **Speed**   (b) **Smells**   (c) **Deep water**   (d) **Loud noises**

5 Which scientist had the space telescope named after him?
(a) **Faraday**   (b) **Darwin**   (c) **Hubble**   (d) **Baird**

6 What do the initials VR stand for in the computer world?
(a) **Very rare**   (b) **Variable risk**   (c) **Virtually redundant**   (d) **Virtual reality**

7 How fast do nerve signals travel to the brain?
(a) **10 metres/sec**   (b) **120 metres/sec**   (c) **4000 m/sec**   (d) **1 metre/sec**

8 What do we call a large group of stars?
(a) **Galaxy**   (b) **Superfamily**   (c) **Maxicluster**   (d) **Supernova**

9 In what field of science is Charles Babbage famous?
(a) **Steam engines**   (b) **Gliders**   (c) **Tunnels**   (d) **Computers**

10 What fell on Isaac Newton's head?
(a) **Apple**   (b) **Cat**   (c) **Branch**   (d) **Bucket**

Q10

Quiz 8 score

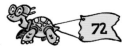

science QUIZ

9

Q9

Your answer

Book answer

1 What is charcoal made from?
(a) **Bones**   (b) **Rock**   (c) **Seaweed**   (d) **Wood**

2 What kind of machine is a combine?
(a) **Plane**   (b) **Tank**   (c) **Harvester**   (d) **Crane**

Q4

3 What do we call the tiny switching devices used in electronics?
(a) **Resisters**   (b) **Transistors**   (c) **Insisters**   (d) **Valves**

4 What tool makes a hole as it twists?
(a) **Chisel**   (b) **Wrench**   (c) **Mallet**   (d) **Drill**

5 Which element has the chemical name H_2O?
(a) **Water**   (b) **Iron**   (c) **Carbon**   (d) **Gold**

6 What kind of substances are oxygen and hydrogen?
(a) **Solids**   (b) **Mixtures**   (d) **Minerals**   (d) **Gases**

Q2

7 What kind of engine could be 2-stroke or 4-stroke?
(a) **Donkey-wheel**   (b) **Windmill**   (c) **Waterwheel**   (d) **Petrol engine**

8 What kind of food are potatoes?
(a) **Carbohydrates**   (b) **Fats**   (c) **Sugars**   (d) **Oils**

9 What medicines do doctors give us to treat infections?
(a) **Antibiotics**   (b) **Antigens**   (c) **Antifreeze**   (d) **Antiseptics**

10 What invention sent messages in Morse code?
(a) **Kinetograph**   (b) **Telegraph**   (c) **Battery**   (d) **Stagecoach**

Quiz 9 score

science QUIZ 10

Q10

		Your answer	Book answer

1
What has a shutter, a lens and a flash?
(a) **Camera** (b) **CD player** (c) **Telescope** (d) **Calculator**

Q1

2
How long does it take the Moon to travel around the Earth?
(a) **12 months** (b) **1 month** (c) **1 day** (d) **7 days**

3
Anything that allows electricity to pass through it easily is a good … what?
(a) **Conductor** (b) **Insulator** (c) **Objector** (d) **Condenser**

4
In engineering, what is a flat-sided object twisted onto a bolt?
(a) **Nib** (b) **Screw** (c) **Pin** (d) **Nut**

5
Where would you find reflecting glass cats' eyes?
(a) **On an airliner** (b) **In an aquarium** (c) **On the road** (d) **On a lighthouse**

6
What produces power by hydroelectricity?
(a) **Ice** (b) **Water** (c) **Sunlight** (d) **Rubbish**

7
Where are a person's taste buds?
(a) **Tongue** (b) **Nose** (c) **Ears** (d) **Fingertips**

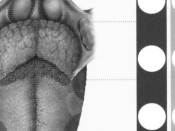
Q7

8
Which is the biggest planet in the Solar System?
(a) **Earth** (b) **Jupiter** (c) **Saturn** (d) **Uranus**

9
Where is your longest bone, the femur?
(a) **Arm** (b) **Thigh** (c) **Spine** (b) **Calf**

10
What was the first people-carrying balloon (1783) filled with?
(a) **Helium gas** (b) **Hydrogen gas** (c) **Feathers** (d) **Hot air**

Quiz 10 score

74

science QUIZ

11

Q6

		Your answer	Book answer

1 Which planet is named after an ancient sea god?
(a) **Neptune** (b) **Mars** (c) **Pluto** (d) **Venus**

2 What is the Sun made of?
(a) **Iron** (b) **Hot gases** (c) **Dust** (d) **Uranium**

Q1

3 What covers 71 percent of the Earth's surface?
(a) **Grass** (b) **Rock** (c) **Sand** (d) **Water**

4 What do we call a mixture of sugar in water?
(a) **Element** (b) **Electrolyte** (c) **Solution** (d) **Honey**

5 Where can you easily feel your pulse?
(a) **Finger** (b) **Wrist** (c) **Knee** (d) **Elbow**

6 What do we call the Sun's family of planets?
(a) **Universe** (b) **Cosmos** (c) **Heavens** (d) **Solar System**

Q8

7 Where are your biceps muscles?
(a) **Eyelid** (b) **Bottom** (c) **Arm** (d) **Leg**

8 What kind of machine has boosters and stages?
(a) **Submarine** (b) **Lift** (c) **Rocket** (d) **Balloon**

9 What goes through your windpipe, or trachea?
(a) **Air** (b) **Blood** (c) **Urine** (d) **Food**

10 In which science did James Clerk Maxwell do important work?
(a) **Medicine** (b) **Physics** (c) **Space research** (d) **Conservation**

Quiz 11 score

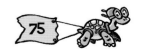

75

science QUIZ 12

Q3

 1 Where in your body is the iris?
(a) **Ear**   (b) **Intestine**   (c) **Brain**   (d) **Eye**

 2 What does the Earth have that no other planet has?
(a) **Air**   (b) **Gravity**   (c) **A moon**   (d) **A spinning motion**

 3 What is another name for a meteor?
(a) **Fiery star**   (b) **Shooting star**   (c) **UFO**   (d) **Comet**

Q4

 4 What kind of machine is a monorail?
(a) **Train**   (b) **Ship**   (c) **Spacecraft**   (d) **Computer**

 5 What does a nurse take your temperature with?
(a) **Stethoscope**   (b) **Tape measure**   (c) **Thermometer**   (d) **Test tube**

 6 What do you count with on an abacus?
(a) **Keys**   (b) **Rods**   (c) **Sticks**   (d) **Beads**

 7 Who was Tycho Brahe?
(a) **Astronomer**   (b) **Chemist**   (c) **Nuclear physicist**   (d) **Inventor**

 8 What are the holes in the Moon called?
(a) **Cracks**   (b) **Craters**   (c) **Crevices**   (d) **Crannies**

 9 What did Gutenberg first do in the 1400s?
(a) **Ride a bike**   (b) **Fly**   (c) **Print by machine**   (d) **Split the atom**
Q6

 10 What is the Earth's outer shell of rock called?
(a) **Bark**   (b) **Mantle**   (c) **Lava**   (d) **Crust**

Quiz 12 score

Science QUIZ

13

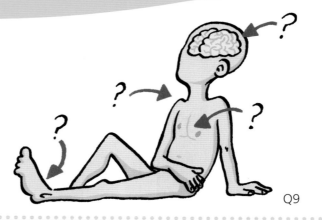

Q9

Your answer **Book answer**

 1 Which planet is known as the Red Planet?
(a) **Pluto**　(b) **Mars**　(c) **Mercury**　(d) **Saturn**

 2 What useful machine did Alexander Graham Bell invent?
(a) **Toilet**　(b) **Toaster**　(c) **Telephone**　(d) **Typewriter**

Q2

 3 In what way does sound travel?
(a) **Trickles**　(b) **Waves**　(c) **Lines**　(d) **Zigzags**

 4 What kind of machine has a clutch and gears?
(a) **Car**　(b) **Glider**　(c) **Yacht**　(d) **Surfboard**

 5 What do scientists measure star-distances in?
(a) **Eons**　(b) **Light-years**　(c) **Kilometres**　(d) **Megamiles**

 6 Which Italian-born inventor invented radio?
(a) **Volta**　(b) **Galileo**　(c) **Galvani**　(d) **Marconi**

Q8

 7 Which planet is closest to the Sun?
(a) **Mercury**　(b) **Venus**　(c) **Mars**　(d) **Earth**

 8 Which of these machines helps us to count?
(a) **Compass**　(b) **Screwpress**　(c) **Dynamo**　(d) **Calculator**

 9 Where in your body is the cerebellum?
(a) **Shoulder**　(b) **Brain**　(c) **Ankle**　(d) **Chest**

 10 Which artist of the 1400s drew flying machines and tanks?
(a) **Michelangelo**　(b) **Leonardo Da Vinci**　(c) **Raphael**　(d) **Titian**

Quiz 13 score

Science QUIZ

14

Q3

		Your answer	Book answer

 1 What is the hottest planet?
(a) **Saturn** (b) **Mars** (c) **Venus** (d) **Mercury**

Q1

 2 What does a scientist measure with a barometer?
(a) **Temperature** (b) **Air pressure** (c) **Ocean depth** (d) **Mountains**

 3 What can be made by twisting plant fibres together?
(a) **Cloth** (b) **Plastic** (c) **Rope** (d) **Spaghetti**

 4 To which science is Andreas Vesalius linked?
(a) **Botany** (b) **Anatomy** (c) **Electronics** (d) **Chemistry**

 5 What do we call the 30,000 mini-planets orbiting the Sun?
(a) **Asteroids** (b) **Comets** (c) **Meteorites** (d) **Infinitesimals**

 6 What machines did Daimler and Benz invent?
(a) **Planes** (b) **CD players** (c) **Cars** (d) **Rockets**

 7 What does a biologist study?
(a) **Gases** (b) **Living things** (c) **Rocks** (d) **Stars**

Q3

 8 Which space traveller has a fiery tail?
(a) **Nebula** (b) **Galaxy** (c) **Comet** (d) **Meteorite**

 9 What does an electromagnet need to make it work?
(a) **Water** (b) **Heat** (c) **Electric current** (d) **Air**

 10 Which parts of your body have a root and a crown?
(a) **Nails** (b) **Teeth** (c) **Hair** (d) **Skin**

Quiz 14 score

science QUIZ

15

Q10

 1 Which metal goes up and down inside a thermometer?
(a) **Mercury**   (b) **Lead**   (c) **Sodium**   (d) **Manganese**

 2 Where is the biggest muscle in your body?
(a) **Chest**   (b) **Stomach**   (c) **Buttocks**   (d) **Leg**

Q5

 3 What made washing clothes easier after 1916?
(a) **Detergents**   (b) **Washing machine**   (c) **Soap**   (d) **Water softener**

 4 What is another name for exercise to music?
(a) **Aerobics**   (b) **Acupuncture**   (c) **Gymnastics**   (d) **Hypnosis**

 5 What machine did Orville and Wilbur Wright travel in for the first time?
(a) **Spacecraft**   (b) **Steam car**   (c) **Electric train**   (d) **Aeroplane**

 6 What is another name for your belly button?
(a) **Nape**   (b) **Funnybone**   (c) **Achilles heel**   (d) **Navel**

 7 Gatling and Maxim gave their names to what inventions?
(a) **Fountain pens**   (b) **Machine guns**   (c) **Engines**   (d) **Steamships**

 8 Which Swedish inventor founded prizes for science?
(a) **Einstein**   (b) **Nobel**   (c) **Mach**   (d) **Oppenheimer**

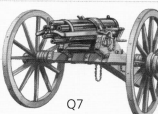

 9 What is at the centre of an atom?
(a) **Nucleus**   (b) **Proton**   (c) **Neutron**   (d) **Electron**

Q7

 10 Which 19th-century naturalist had ideas about evolution?
(a) **Scott**   (b) **Attenborough**   (c) **Darwin**   (d) **Leakey**

Quiz 15 score

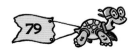

Science QUIZ

16

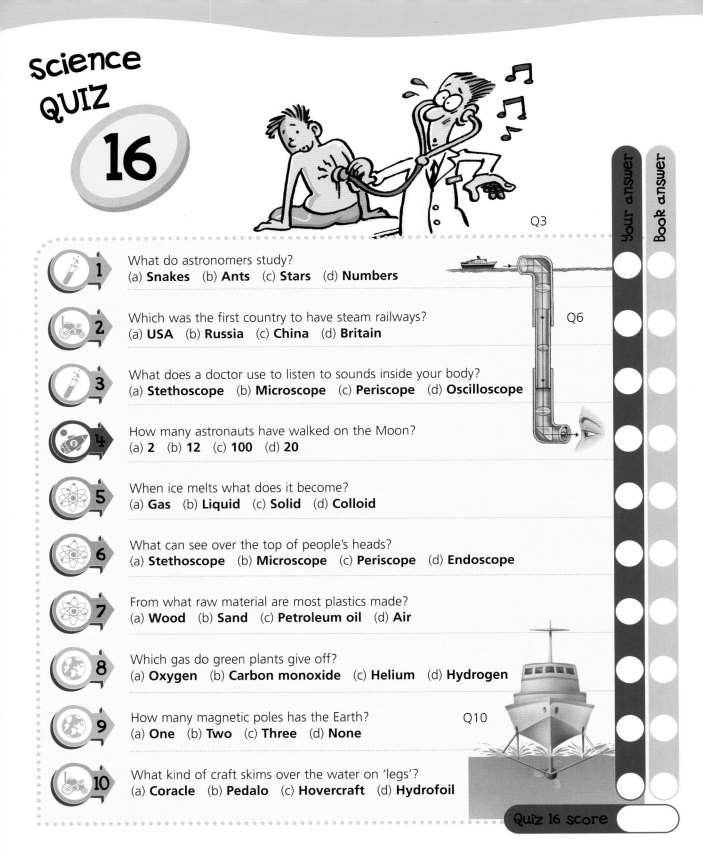

	Your answer	Book answer

1 What do astronomers study?
(a) **Snakes** (b) **Ants** (c) **Stars** (d) **Numbers**

2 Which was the first country to have steam railways?
(a) **USA** (b) **Russia** (c) **China** (d) **Britain**

3 What does a doctor use to listen to sounds inside your body?
(a) **Stethoscope** (b) **Microscope** (c) **Periscope** (d) **Oscilloscope**

4 How many astronauts have walked on the Moon?
(a) **2** (b) **12** (c) **100** (d) **20**

5 When ice melts what does it become?
(a) **Gas** (b) **Liquid** (c) **Solid** (d) **Colloid**

6 What can see over the top of people's heads?
(a) **Stethoscope** (b) **Microscope** (c) **Periscope** (d) **Endoscope**

7 From what raw material are most plastics made?
(a) **Wood** (b) **Sand** (c) **Petroleum oil** (d) **Air**

8 Which gas do green plants give off?
(a) **Oxygen** (b) **Carbon monoxide** (c) **Helium** (d) **Hydrogen**

9 How many magnetic poles has the Earth?
(a) **One** (b) **Two** (c) **Three** (d) **None**

10 What kind of craft skims over the water on 'legs'?
(a) **Coracle** (b) **Pedalo** (c) **Hovercraft** (d) **Hydrofoil**

Q3

Q6

Q10

Quiz 16 score

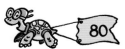

science QUIZ

17

Q1

1 What is solid water called?
(a) **Vapour** (b) **Steam** (c) **Ice** (d) **Moisture**

2 How long does a human baby grow inside its mother?
(a) **12 months** (b) **24 months** (c) **9 months** (d) **6 months**

3 Which was the last planet to be discovered, in 1930?
(a) **Mars** (b) **Saturn** (c) **Neptune** (d) **Pluto**

Q3

4 What does the H in H-bomb stand for?
(a) **Helium** (b) **Hydrogen** (c) **Heavy water** (d) **Horrendous**

5 Coal is a form of what element?
(a) **Iron** (b) **Carbon** (c) **Oxygen** (d) **Sodium**

Q7

6 What do geologists study?
(a) **Clouds** (b) **Rocks** (c) **Bugs** (d) **Diseases**

7 Which supersonic plane made farewell flights in 2003?
(a) **Tu-144** (b) **Shuttle** (c) **Airbus** (d) **Concorde**

8 Where are the Van Allen Belts?
(a) **Around the Earth** (b) **On the Moon** (c) **Around Saturn** (d) **On Mars**

9 What did Dr Barnard transplant in 1967?
(a) **A head** (b) **A heart** (c) **A cloned tomato** (d) **An arm**

10 In 1662, Robert Boyle drew up laws describing what?
(a) **Gases** (b) **Gravity** (c) **Water** (d) **Heat**

Quiz 17 score

science QUIZ

18

Q8

1 What is a monsoon?
(a) **A tidal wave** (b) **A snake-killing animal** (c) **A wind** (d) **A star**

2 What's another name for a reflected sound?
(a) **Ripple** (b) **Murmur** (c) **Chime** (d) **Echo**

Q7

3 At what temperature does water boil?
(a) **10°C** (b) **80°C** (c) **100°C** (d) **212°C**

4 What can be measured by Mach numbers?
(a) **Pressure** (b) **Aircraft speed** (c) **Sweetness** (d) **Loudness**

5 What have *Saturn*, *Titan*, *Long March* and *Ariane* in common?
(a) **All cars** (b) **All planets** (c) **All rockets** (d) **All diseases**

6 Acoustics is the study of what?
(a) **Trees** (b) **Manners** (c) **Sounds** (d) **Plastics**

7 Which of these did Thomas Edison not invent?
(a) **Power station** (b) **Light bulb** (c) **Phonograph** (d) **Car**

Q5

8 What sort of scientist was Johannes Kepler?
(a) **Biologist** (b) **Engineer** (c) **Naturalist** (d) **Astronomer**

9 Which of these gives the Earth heat and light?
(a) **Sun** (b) **Moon** (c) **Mars** (d) **Jupiter**

10 What natural material is paper made from?
(a) **Oil** (b) **Wood** (c) **Sand** (d) **Grass**

Quiz 18 score

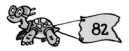

science QUIZ

19

Q8

 1 What does an entomologist study?
(a) **Insects**   (b) **Birds**   (c) **Fish**   (d) **Icicles**

 2 Which machine can be controlled by a mouse?
(a) **Washing machine**   (b) **Computer**   (c) **Lawnmower**   (d) **Strimmer**

 3 What did the Lumière brothers show for the first time in 1896?
(a) **Skeletons**   (b) **Colour TV**   (c) **Cinema films**   (d) **Electric light**

 4 What is heard when a plane breaks the 'sound barrier'?
(a) **Nothing**   (b) **A whistle**   (c) **Music**   (d) **Sonic boom**

 5 What makes a spacecraft glow as it re-enters the atmosphere?
(a) **Turbulence**   (b) **Pressure**   (c) **Friction**   (d) **Dust**

Q6

 6 What is another name for an earthquake-made tidal wave?
(a) **Waterfall**   (b) **Tsunami**   (c) **Hurricane**   (d) **Cyclone**

 7 What do the initials VHS have to do with?
(a) **Videotape**   (b) **CDs**   (c) **Microwaves**   (d) **Laptops**

 8 What kind of machine has rotor blades?
(a) **Bicycle**   (b) **Razor**   (c) **Fridge**   (d) **Helicopter**

 9 Which of these helps you to draw straight lines?
(a) **Protractor**   (b) **Compasses**   (c) **Ruler**   (d) **Rubber**

Q7

 10 What do we call a room for science experiments?
(a) **Lavatory**   (b) **Greenhouse**   (c) **Toolroom**   (d) **Laboratory**

Quiz 19 score

science QUIZ 20

Q6

Your answer   Book answer

1 Botany is the study of what?
(a) **Bodies** (b) **Australia** (c) **Flies** (d) **Plants**

2 If a plane is flying supersonically what is it doing?
(a) **Landing** (b) **Taking off** (c) **Climbing** (d) **Flying faster than sound**

3 Which of these foods is often sold freeze-dried?
(a) **Bananas** (b) **Coffee** (c) **Lemonade** (d) **Cheese**

4 What does an astronomer study?
(a) **Stars** (b) **Cars** (c) **Plants** (d) **Animals**

Q1

5 What instrument is used to weigh objects?
(a) **Microscope** (b) **Scales** (c) **Binoculars** (d) **Ruler**

6 What does an optician test?
(a) **Your ears** (b) **Your reflexes** (c) **Your lungs** (d) **Your eyes**

7 What tool can be used to bang in and pull out nails?
(a) **Hammer** (b) **Saw** (c) **Pliers** (d) **Spanner**

Q7

8 What did Clarence Birdseye invent in the 1920s?
(a) **Photocopier** (b) **Video camera** (c) **Frozen food** (d) **Binoculars**

9 What did Edward Jenner discover to help fight disease?
(a) **Sticking plaster** (b) **Vaccination** (c) **Disinfectant** (d) **Toilet paper**

10 What travels at 300,000 km a second?
(a) **The Earth** (b) **A satellite** (c) **Light** (d) **Sound**

Quiz 20 score

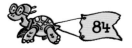

Science QUIZ

21

Q9

Your answer　　**Book answer**

 1 What did Volta invent in 1800 to store electricity?
(a) **Generator** (b) **Magnet** (c) **Plug** (d) **Battery**

 2 What body part does a dermatologist look after?
(a) **Hair** (b) **Skin** (c) **Feet** (d) **Heart**

 3 Which of these absorbs water most easily?
(a) **Wood** (b) **Potato** (c) **Sponge** (d) **Spoon**

 4 Which planet was landed on by Vikings (space probes)?
(a) **Venus** (b) **Jupiter** (c) **Mercury** (d) **Mars**

Q1

 5 What kind of machine was a Colt 45?
(a) **Car** (b) **Gun** (c) **Record** (d) **Mechanical horse**

 6 What did the Egyptians use papyrus for?
(a) **Writing** (b) **Building** (c) **Eating** (d) **Burning**

 7 In which country were skin grafts done 3000 years ago?
(a) **USA** (b) **Brazil** (c) **France** (d) **India**

 8 What did Lewis Waterman invent to make letter-writing easier?
(a) **Typewriter** (b) **Blotting paper** (c) **Fountain pen** (d) **Palm pilot**

 9 Which of these will a magnet not pick up?
(a) **Nail** (b) **Pin** (c) **Paper Clip** (d) **Rubber**

 10 Which organs in the body filter the blood?
(a) **Ears** (b) **Lungs** (c) **Testes** (d) **Kidneys**

Q8

Quiz 21 score

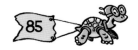 85

science QUIZ

22

Q5

Your answer   Book answer

 1 Who or what does a paedatrician look after?
(a) **Animals**   (b) **Plants**   (c) **Old buildings**   (d) **Sick children**

 2 Which instrument tells a builder a surface is level?
(a) **Balance scales**   (b) **Spirit level**   (c) **Set square**   (d) **Plumb line**

 3 How many breaths does a person take in a lifetime?
(a) **100 million**   (b) **600 million**   (c) **350 million**   (d) **1000 million**

 4 What are the ends of a magnet called?
(a) **Ends**   (b) **Terminals**   (c) **Poles**   (d) **Cathodes**

Q5

 5 What kind of craft rides on a cushion of air?
(a) **Hovercraft**   (b) **Hydrofoil**   (c) **Yacht**   (d) **Dinghy**

 6 Which device changes sound into electric signals?
(a) **Mouse**   (b) **Microphone**   (c) **Ear-trumpet**   (d) **Battery**

Q7

 7 What did Hans Lippershey first look through in 1608?
(a) **Keyhole**   (b) **Magnifying glass**   (c) **Glasses**   (d) **Telescope**

 8 Daguerre and Eastman are famous for inventing what?
(a) **Steam trains**   (b) **Balloons**   (c) **Photography**   (d) **Electricity**

 9 In what industry was the spinning jenny an important invention?
(a) **Textiles**   (b) **Coal mining**   (c) **Sound recording**   (d) **Glass making**

 10 To what did Anders Celsius give his name?
(a) **Temperature scale**   (b) **Pressure gauge**   (c) **Planet**   (d) **Kind of rock**

Quiz 22 score

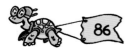

science QUIZ

23

1 What was Stephenson's Rocket?
(a) **Spacecraft**   (b) **Boat**   (c) **Steam locomotive**   (d) **Car**

Q3

2 What do we call the thin wire inside a light bulb?
(a) **Element**   (b) **Electrode**   (c) **Fuse**   (d) **Filament**

Q1

3 What machine lifts heavy goods in a factory or warehouse?
(a) **Forklift**   (b) **Tractor**   (c) **Conveyor**   (d) **Supercharger**

4 Who might use a theodolite in their work?
(a) **A chemist**   (b) **A surveyor**   (c) **A doctor**   (d) **A farmer**

5 If a mother has triplets, how many babies are there?
(a) **Two**   (b) **Three**   (c) **Four**   (d) **Six**

6 What is zoology the study of?
(a) **Zoos**   (b) **Animals**   (c) **Words**   (d) **Diseases**

Q6

7 Where would you find a crater and a lava chamber?
(a) **Laboratory**   (b) **Volcano**   (c) **Moon**   (d) **Ants' nest**

8 Which is the most abundant element on Earth?
(a) **Hydrogen**   (b) **Oxygen**   (c) **Water**   (d) **Sodium**

9 Which of these is a way heat can move?
(a) **Convection**   (b) **Insulation**   (c) **Adaptation**   (d) **Condensation**

10 What can travel around the Earth seven times in less than a second?
(a) **Air**   (b) **Satellite**   (c) **Meteor**   (d) **Light**

Quiz 23 score

Science QUIZ

24

Q4

1 Which part of your body has valves?
(a) **Brain** (b) **Heart** (c) **Liver** (d) **Knee**

Q5

2 What is the study of the mind and mental processes?
(a) **Dentistry** (b) **Psychology** (c) **Physics** (d) **Surgery**

3 What unit measures electrical resistance?
(a) **Litre** (b) **Kilogram** (c) **Ohm** (d) **Gallon**

4 What is the change that an insect goes through as it grows?
(a) **Evolution** (b) **Decay** (c) **Metamorphosis** (d) **Crystallization**

5 Which part of your body fills with air every time you breathe in?
(a) **Lungs** (b) **Skull** (c) **Nose** (d) **Heart**

6 What is another term for rust?
(a) **Corrosion** (b) **Dehydration** (c) **Erosion** (d) **Suspension**

7 What was *Sputnik 1*?
(a) **Asteroid** (b) **Manned spacecraft** (c) **Satellite** (d) **Rocket**

8 Who first showed that the Earth moved around the Sun?
(a) **Archimedes** (b) **Bacon** (c) **Copernicus** (d) **Newton**

9 Which Polish scientist discovered radium?
(a) **Einstein** (b) **Curie** (c) **Rutherford** (d) **Marconi**

10 Which device changes electrical signals back into sounds?
(a) **Plug** (b) **Eardrum** (c) **Valve** (d) **Loudspeaker**

Q9

Quiz 24 score

science QUIZ

25

Q9

1 Apollo, Mercury and Vostok were all what?
(a) **Satellites** (b) **Manned spacecraft** (c) **Astronauts** (d) **Giant fireworks**

2 Where in your body is the retina?
(a) **Brain** (b) **Heart** (c) **Eye** (d) **Stomach**

Q4

3 What kind of lamps did people have in ancient Greece?
Gas (a) **Oil** (b) **Electric** (c) **None** (d)

4 Suspension and cantilever are two kinds of what?
(a) **Cranes** (b) **Trucks** (c) **Guns** (d) **Bridges**

5 Who was the first scientist to look into space through a telescope?
(a) **Pythagoras** (b) **Darwin** (c) **Galileo** (d) **Goddard**

6 In which female body organ does a baby develop before birth?
(a) **Breast** (b) **Appendix** (c) **Bowel** (d) **Womb**

7 What do scientists study from an observatory?
(a) **Earthquakes** (b) **Wildlife** (c) **Pollution** (d) **The stars**

8 Which organ of the body stores urine?
(a) **Liver** (b) **Bladder** (c) **Spleen** (d) **Tonsil**

9 Roman horsemen rode without what useful invention?
(a) **Saddle** (b) **Reins** (c) **Boots** (d) **Stirrups**

Q5

10 What does a chronometer do?
(a) **Tell the time** (b) **Count chromosomes** (c) **Weigh things** (d) **Record speed**

Quiz 25 score

science QUIZ 26

 1 What was Neil Armstrong the first man to do in 1969?
(a) **Climb Everest**   (b) **Walk on the Moon**   (c) **Fly supersonic**   (d) **Skydive**

 2 Which scientist sat in a bath to measure gold?
(a) **Archimedes**   (b) **Einstein**   (c) **Davy**   (d) **Whittle**

 3 What were sundials and sandglasses used to measure?
(a) **Distance**   (b) **Heat**   (c) **Time**   (d) **Density**

 4 Which animals use ultrasound to navigate?
(a) **Snails**   (b) **Dolphins**   (c) **Worms**   (d) **Camels**

Q4

 5 The Bell X-1 (1947) was the first … what?
(a) **Telephone**   (b) **Laptop**   (c) **Colour TV**   (d) **Supersonic plane**

 6 How many muscles do you have?
(a) **About 100**   (b) **About 640**   (c) **About 1000**   (d) **About 10,000**

 7 What did John Smeaton build around Britain's coasts?
(a) **Ships**   (b) **Lighthouses**   (c) **Breakwaters**   (d) **Piers**

 8 How many wings has a biplane?
(a) **None**   (b) **One**   (c) **Two**   (d) **Four**   Q7

 9 Where would you find the Sea of Tranquility and the Bay of Storms?
(a) **Earth**   (b) **Moon**   (c) **Mars**   (d) **Venus**

 10 What did Alfred Nobel invent that made a big bang?
(a) **Fireworks**   (b) **Dynamite**   (c) **TNT**   (d) **Atomic bomb**

Your answer   Book answer

Quiz 26 score

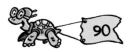

science QUIZ

27

Q7

 1 Which American discovered lightning was electricity?
(a) **Washington** (b) **Lincoln** (c) **Edison** (d) **Franklin**

Q1

 2 Which parts of a car engine go up and down inside cylinders?
(a) **Pistons** (b) **Valves** (c) **Brake pads** (d) **Gears**

 3 Which winged spacecraft first flew in 1981?
(a) **Concorde** (b) **Ariane** (c) **Space Shuttle** (d) **Apollo**

 4 What do we call the rebound of sound and light from a surface?
(a) **Rejection** (b) **Reflection** (c) **Absorption** (d) **Reincarnation**

 5 Which of these is not a form of carbon?
(a) **Soot** (b) **Charcoal** (c) **Diamond** (d) **Chalk**

 6 Roughly how many chemical elements are there in nature?
(a) **About 50** (b) **About 350** (c) **About 100** (d) **About 200**

 7 By what process do plants make food?
(a) **Photosynthesis** (b) **Photoelectricity** (c) **Biorhythm** (d) **Pollination**

 8 The Simplon (1905) was the world's longest … what?
(a) **Rail tunnel** (b) **Dam** (c) **Rollercoaster** (d) **Train**

Q10

 9 A habitat plus its animals and plants is a … what?
(a) **Resource** (b) **Ecosystem** (c) **Species** (d) **Order**

 10 What kind of machine was a penny farthing?
(a) **Slot machine** (b) **Shop till** (c) **Bicycle** (d) **Car**

Quiz 27 score

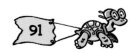

science QUIZ

28

Q3

 1 Which French scientist showed how bacteria makes food go bad?
(a) **Pascal**　(b) **Papin**　(c) **Pasteur**　(d) **Cantona**

 2 What happens to an iron nail left in water?
(a) **It rusts**　(b) **It dissolves**　(c) **It melts**　(d) **It gets longer**

 3 Which poisonous gas comes out of car exhausts?
(a) **Nitrogen**　(b) **Oxygen**　(c) **Carbon monoxide**　(d) **Helium**

 4 Which reddish metal is good for making electrical wires?
(a) **Iron**　(b) **Copper**　(c) **Lead**　(d) **Gold**

 5 What do we call the hardened remains of a long-dead animal?
(a) **Fissure**　(b) **Compost**　(c) **Relic**　(d) **Fossil**

 6 What colour is the mineral ruby?
(a) **Green**　(b) **Blue**　(c) **Red**　(d) **White**

Q6

 7 On which continent was the hottest temperature measured (58°C)?
(a) **Africa**　(b) **North America**　(c) **Europe**　(d) **Antarctica**

 8 Which planet has the biggest and brightest rings?
(a) **Jupiter**　(b) **Saturn**　(c) **Mars**　(d) **Neptune**

 9 Who were first to use the magnetic compass?
(a) **Chinese**　(b) **Egyptians**　(c) **Romans**　(d) **Aztecs**

Q9

 10 Which is the most common solvent?
(a) **Milk**　(b) **Water**　(c) **Olive oil**　(d) **Sand**

Quiz 28 score

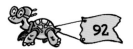

Chart Your Scores

Science	1	2	3	4	5	6	7	8	9	10
Quiz 1										
Quiz 2										
Quiz 3										
Quiz 4										
Quiz 5										
Quiz 6										
Quiz 7										
Quiz 8										
Quiz 9										
Quiz 10										
Quiz 11										
Quiz 12										
Quiz 13										
Quiz 14										
Quiz 15										
Quiz 16										
Quiz 17										
Quiz 18										
Quiz 19										
Quiz 20										
Quiz 21										
Quiz 22										
Quiz 23										
Quiz 24										
Quiz 25										
Quiz 26										
Quiz 27										
Quiz 28										

History

Key to subject icons

 Ancient history

 Revolutions and discoveries

 Famous people

 Rulers and conquerors

 Everyday life and times

 Modern history

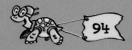

History
QUIZ

1

| | Your answer | Book answer |

 1 What disaster destroyed Pompeii in AD79?
(a) **Asteroid**   (b) **Flood**   (c) **Volcano**   (d) **Tidal wave**

Q4

 2 Who was the first British monarch to travel in a train?
(a) **Victoria**   (b) **Edward VII**   (c) **George IV**   (d) **Charles II**

 3 For what was Hans Holbein famous in Tudor times?
(a) **Explorer**   (b) **Executioner**   (c) **Rebel**   (d) **Painter**

 4 With which queen did Julius Caesar and Mark Antony fall in love?
(a) **Victoria**   (b) **Boudicca**   (c) **Cleopatra**   (d) **Alexandra**

 5 In which country did Ned Kelly become an outlaw?
(a) **USA**   (b) **Britain**   (c) **Ireland**   (d) **Australia**

Q7

 6 Which country used to be led by rulers called tsars?
(a) **China**   (b) **Russia**   (c) **Brazil**   (d) **Sweden**

 7 What would Ice Age people have hunted?
(a) **Pythons**   (b) **Giant tortoises**   (c) **Woolly mammoths**   (d) **Giraffes**

 8 On which Mediterranean island was Napoleon Bonaparte born?
(a) **Crete**   (b) **Sardinia**   (c) **Cyprus**   (d) **Corsica**

 9 Was Elizabeth Fry…?
(a) **Prison reformer**   (b) **Pirate**   (c) **Chocolate maker**   (d) **Explorer**

 10 Of which revolution was Robespierre a leader?
(a) **Glorious**   (b) **American**   (c) **Cuban**   (d) **French**

Quiz 1 score

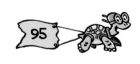

95

History QUIZ

2

Your answer   Book answer

1 By what name was the outlaw William Bonney better known?
(a) **Billy the Kid**   (b) **Jesse James**   (c) **Buffalo Bill**   (d)**Sundance Kid**

2 What was President Lincoln's first name?
(a) **Albert**   (b) **George**   (c) **William**   (d) **Abraham**

3 Which French ruler built the Palace of Versailles?
(a) **Louis XIV**   (b) **Henry IV**   (c) **General de Gaulle**   (d) **Jacques Chirac**

4 Which ancient civilization created the Sphinx and the Pyramids?
(a) **Egyptian**   (b) **Maya**   (c) **Persian**   (d) **Aztec**

Q4

5 Who made his first car in 1893?
(a) **Henry Ford**   (b) **Louis Blériot**   (c) **Wilbur Wright**   (d) **John Logie Baird**

6 Which country was the centre of the Inca civilization?
(a) **Canada**   (b) **Peru**   (c) **Pakistan**   (d) **England**

7 Which country used to have an emperor called the kaiser?
(a) **France**   (b) **Russia**   (c) **Italy**   (d) **Germany**

8 For what crime was Dr Crippen executed in 1910?
(a) **Treason**   (b) **Spying**   (c) **Murder**   (d) **Train-wrecking**

Q10

9 How many children had Queen Elizabeth I?
(a) **One**   (b) **Four**   (c) **Two**   (d) **None**

10 Who tried to blow up the British Houses of Parliament in 1605?
(a) **James I**   (b) **Guy Fawkes**   (c) **Philip II**   (d) **Titus Oates**

Quiz 2 score

History QUIZ

3

Q5

1 Who is the patron saint of Ireland?
(a) **David** (b) **Patrick** (c) **George** (d) **Andrew**

2 Who did Queen Elizabeth I of England marry?
(a) **Philip of Spain** (b) **Earl of Leicester** (c) **No one** (d) **Duke of Alencon**

3 Of which country was Helmut Kohl leader until 1998?
(a) **Russia** (b) **Germany** (c) **France** (d) **USA**

Q4

4 Which Indian leader was known as the Mahatma or Great Soul?
(a) **Nehru** (b) **Buddha** (c) **Babur** (d) **Gandhi**

5 What kind of craft were Zeppelins?
(a) **Submarines** (b) **Airships** (c) **Jets** (d) **Rockets**

Q6

6 What were *Locomotion No 1* and *Puffing Billy*?
(a) **Early tanks** (b) **Steamships** (c) **Steam trains** (d) **Early planes**

7 *The Heinkel 178* (1938) was the world's first … what?
(a) **Television set** (b) **Steamship** (c) **Jet plane** (d) **Satellite**

8 What did 19th-century doctors use ether for?
(a) **Anaesthetic** (b) **Antiseptic** (c) **Cough mixture** (d) **Plastering broken bones**

9 Which event happened in 1381?
(a) **Battle of Britain** (b) **Peasants' Revolt** (c) **Irish Famine** (c) **Julius Caesar died**

10 What did John Dunlop invent for his son's tricycle?
(a) **Saddle** (b) **Air-filled tyres** (c) **Brakes** (d) **Gears**

Quiz 3 score

History QUIZ 4

Q10

1 What did John McAdam improve in Britain?
(a) **Roads**   (b) **Railways**   (c) **Canals**   (d) **Drains**

2 Which household invention was first plugged in in 1901?
(a) **Electric iron**   (b) **Washing machine**   (c) **Vacuum cleaner**   (d) **TV**

3 What did the Romans use for central heating?
(a) **Natural gas**   (b) **Coke**   (c) **Candles**   (d) **Hot air**

Q2

4 Which country was ruled by shoguns?
(a) **Japan**   (b) **China**   (c) **Nigeria**   (d) **Mexico**

5 Which ancient Chinese medical treatment gives people the needle?
(a) **Acupuncture**   (b) **Hypnosis**   (c) **Aromatherapy**   (d) **Massage**

6 How were bricks dried in the ancient world?
(a) **Gas**   (b) **Coal**   (c) **Sun**   (d) **Electricity**

Q5

7 Who was Britain's first prime minister, in 1721?
(a) **Walpole**   (b) **Pitt**   (c) **Gladstone**   (d) **Heath**

8 Which woman scientist won two Nobel prizes?
(a) **Curie**   (b) **Nightingale**   (c) **Anderson**   (d) **Pankhurst**

9 Which group of Americans went to Great Salt Lake, USA, in 1847?
(a) **Apache**   (b) **Mormons**   (c) **Puritans**   (d) **Mountain men**

10 Where did Victorian ladies wear a crinoline?
(a) **Head**   (b) **Feet**   (c) **Underskirt**   (d) **On finger**

Quiz 4 score

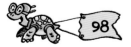

History QUIZ

5

Q7

| | Your answer | Book answer |

1 In which city did the Jack the Ripper murders take place?
(a) **New York** (b) **Paris** (c) **Edinburgh** (d) **London**

2 What did Colonel Blood try to steal in 1671?
(a) **London Bridge** (b) **Stone of Scone** (c) **Crown Jewels** (d) **Magna Carta**

3 What were both Benedict Arnold and Mata Hari?
(a) **Explorers** (b) **Spies** (c) **Aviators** (d) **Inventors**

Q2

4 Which of these cities had a Viking settlement?
(a) **New York** (b) **Canberra** (c) **Dublin** (d) **Rome**

5 What was the nickname of the US Civil War general Thomas Jackson?
(a) **Blood and Guts** (b) **Ironface** (c) **Stonewall** (d) **Old Tom**

6 Which king ordered Domesday Book to be made in England?
(a) **William I** (b) **Edward I** (c) **Henry VIII** (d) **George III**

7 Who is said to have put his cloak in a puddle for a queen to walk on?
(a) **Shakespeare** (b) **Raleigh** (c) **Dickens** (d) **Cromwell**

Q9

8 In which war were Haig and Pershing famous commanders?
(a) **Boer War** (b) **Crimean War** (c) **World War I** (d) **Iraq War**

9 What did Wilberforce campaign to end in the 19th century?
(a) **Child labour** (b) **Slavery** (c) **Fur trade** (d) **Cigarette smoking**

10 What was founded by Robert Baden-Powell?
(a) **Salvation Army** (b) **Boy Scouts** (c) **United Nations** (d) **Greenpeace**

Quiz 5 score

99

History QUIZ

6

Q8

 1 Where was the empire ruled by Akbar the Great?
(a) **China**   (b) **Persia**   (c) **Egypt**   (d) **India**

 2 Which ocean did Charles Lindbergh fly across in 1927?
(a) **Pacific**   (b) **North Sea**   (c) **Atlantic**   (d) **Indian**

 3 Who was the first president of the United States?
(a) **Jefferson**   (b) **Franklin**   (c) **Washington**   (d) **Kennedy**

 4 In which decade were tea bags first used?
(a) **1840s**   (b) **1870s**   (c) **1920s**   (d) **1970s**

Q5

 5 What did a Hungarian named Biro invent in the 1940s?
(a) **Jet plane**   (b) **Ballpoint pen**   (c) **TV**   (d) **Radar**

 6 Which of these came first?
(a) **Jeans**   (b) **Zip fastener**   (c) **Jumbo jet**   (d) **CD player**

 7 What was a 1940s doodlebug?
(a) **Dance**   (b) **Battleship**   (c) **Flying bomb**   (d) **Tin hat**

Q10

 8 Which explorer was first to reach the South Pole?
(a) **Cook**   (b) **Peary**   (c) **Amundsen**   (d) **Darwin**

 9 By what nickname was the 1969 Moon-walking astronaut Edwin Aldrin known?
(a) **Spider**   (b) **Buzz**   (c) **Pancho**   (d) **Loony**

 10 Which of these people are native to Australia?
(a) **Maori**   (b) **Zulus**   (c) **Arawak**   (d) **Aborigines**

Quiz 6 score

History QUIZ

7

Q6

 1 What kind of boats did Polynesians use for ocean voyages?
(a) **Kayaks**   (b) **Outrigger canoes**   (c) **Coracles**   (d) **Galleys**

 2 For what did Amelia Earhart become famous in the 1930s?
(a) **Films**   (b) **Flying**   (c) **Fast cars**   (d) **Women's rights**

 3 Which scientist showed that the Earth was not the centre of the Universe?
(a) **Bacon**   (b) **Chaucer**   (c) **Copernicus**   (d) **Einstein**

 4 Where did Vasco da Gama sail in 1498?
(a) **America**   (b) **Australia**   (c) **China**   (d) **India**

Q5

 5 Which of these inventions/discoveries came first?
(a) **Clay pots**   (b) **Metal tools**   (c) **Fire**   (d) **Steam power**

 6 Which two countries began a space race in 1957?
(a) **China/Russia**   (b) **USA/Russia**   (c) **Britain/France**   (d) **Germany/France**

 7 Which people were ruled by the Han dynasty?
(a) **Egyptians**   (b) **Japanese**   (c) **Chinese**   (d) **French**

 8 Which country was ruled by the Bourbon royal family?
(a) **Italy**   (b) **France**   (c) **USA**   (d) **Scotland**

 9 Which of these was a spear used by Zulu warriors?
(a) **Halberd**   (b) **Matchlock**   (c) **Assegai**   (d) **Javelin**

Q9

 10 Which country did Mussolini lead in the 20th century?
(a) **Germany**   (b) **Argentina**   (c) **France**   (d) **Italy**

Quiz 7 score

History QUIZ

8

Q5

1 Which weapon did a medieval soldier have to wind up?
(a) **Arquebus**   (b) **Cannon**   (c) **Crossbow**   (d) **Longbow**

2 Who of these was poorest in medieval times?
(a) **Baron**   (b) **Villein**   (c) **Bishop**   (d) **King**   Q1

3 How many wives did Henry VIII have?
(a) **One**   (b) **Three**   (c) **Six**   (d) **Eight**

4 Of what is the mask of Egypt's King Tutankhamun made?
(a) **Gold**   (b) **Paper**   (c) **Plastic**   (d) **Furs**

5 What animal-symbol on his head showed that a pharaoh was ruler of Egypt?
(a) **Bear**   (b) **Tiger**   (c) **Lion**   (d) **Snake**

6 Which of these set out to attack England in 1588?
(a) **Great Armadillo**   (b) **Great Armour**   (c) **Great Armada**   (d) **Great Armful**

7 Genghis Khan was a feared warrior, from which continent?
(a) **Africa**   (b) **Asia**   (c) **South America**   (d) **Europe**

8 Complete the name of this warrior-leader: Attila the …?
(a) **Dreadful**   (b) **Fearsome**   (c) **Hun**   (d) **Handsome**

9 What did men drive when horse racing in Ancient Rome?
(a) **Chariots**   (b) **Cars**   (c) **Go-karts**   (d) **Wagons**

Q5

10 Which Duke led the British to victory at Waterloo?
(a) **Marlborough**   (b) **York**   (c) **Wellington**   (d) **Albermarle**

Your answer

Book answer

Quiz 8 score

History QUIZ

9

		Your answer	Book answer

1 In which country was Adolf Hitler born?
(a) **Germany**   (b) **Austria**   (c) **France**   (d) **Russia**

2 Which of these is an expert on the past?
(a) **Biologist**   (b) **Anatomist**   (c) **Archaeologist**   (d) **Geologist**

3 What did Vikings make from cows' bones?   Q5
(a) **Combs**   (b) **Ice skates**   (c) **Flutes**   (d) **Spears**

4 Who built the Sutton Hoo ship?
(a) **Normans**   (b) **Angles**   (c) **Apaches**   (d) **Franks**

5 Who was the Native American war chief?
(a) **Sitting Bull**   (b) **Hereward the Wake**   (c) **Kublai Khan**   (d) **Prester John**

6 What did the USA buy from Russia in 1867?
(a) **Alaska**   (b) **Canada**   (c) **Siberia**   (d) **Hawaii**   Q2

7 Where did samurai warriors fight?
(a) **India**   (b) **New Zealand**   (c) **Japan**   (d) **South Africa**

8 Where did Roman chariot racing take place?
(a) **Forum**   (b) **Theatre**   (c) **Circus**   (d) **Market**

9 What upset the peace in France in 1789?
(a) **National strike**   (b) **Revolution**   (c) **Plague**   (d) **Earthquake**

10 Who said no to British rule in 1776?
(a) **Scotland**   (b) **America**   (c) **Australia**   (d) **India**

Quiz 9 score

History QUIZ 10

Q2

| | Your answer | Book answer |

1 Where was Simon Bolivar called 'the Liberator'?
(a) **Ireland** (b) **South America** (c) **Canada** (d) **Nigeria**

2 Whose battles included Austerlitz and Marengo?
(a) **Napoleon** (b) **Custer** (c) **Julius Caesar** (d) **Cromwell**

3 Which of these people settled Britain before the Romans?
(a) **Polynesians** (b) **Saxons** (c) **Celts** (d) **Normans**

4 On which continent was the Songhai empire?
(a) **Africa** (b) **Asia** (c) **Europe** (d) **Antarctica**

Q2

5 Where was Cape Colony founded?
(a) **South America** (b) **South Australia** (c) **South Africa** (d) **South Pole**

6 Which country was once called New France?
(a) **Australia** (b) **Canada** (c) **Scotland** (d) **Spain**

7 Who might have worn a helmet and greaves?
(a) **Knight** (b) **Nun** (c) **Queen** (d) **Monk**

Q7

8 What river did Cartier sail up in the 1530s?
(a) **Nile** (b) **St Lawrence** (c) **Ganges** (d) **Volga**

9 Where was Henry the Navigator a prince?
(a) **Portugal** (b) **Morocco** (c) **Ukraine** (d) **Norway**

10 Where did the Guptas rule?
(a) **India** (b) **China** (c) **Japan** (d) **Spain**

Quiz 10 score

History QUIZ
11

Q8

		Your answer	Book answer

 1 What was a dragoon?
(a) **Mythical monster** (b) **Mounted soldier** (c) **Slave** (d) **Hat**

 2 Where was the centre of medieval life in Europe?
(a) **Windmill** (b) **Shops** (c) **Community centre** (d) **Castle**

Q4

 3 What was a flintlock used for?
(a) **Fire bullets** (b) **Dig holes** (c) **Chain prisoners** (d) **Shape stones**

 4 Who fought in a jousting tournament?
(a) **Gladiators** (b) **Knights** (c) **Bandits** (d) **Boxers**

 5 For what were birds of prey used in medieval times?
(a) **Singing contests** (b) **Feathered hats** (c) **Hawking** (d) **Angling**

 6 What was the *Dreadnought* of 1906?
(a) **Battleship** (b) **Tank** (c) **Big gun** (d) **Gas-proof suit**   Q8

 7 Whom did Anne of Cleves and Anne Boleyn both marry?
(a) **Prince Albert** (b) **King John** (c) **King Henry VIII** (d) **Robin Hood**

 8 What did a medieval minstrel do?
(a) **Cure people** (b) **Bake pies** (c) **Hunt deer** (d) **Sing and play music**

 9 Which of these kings is not British?
(a) **Richard III** (b) **James I** (c) **Gustavus Adolphus** (d) **Edward VII**

 10 On which river did the ancient Egyptians depend?
(a) **Amazon** (b) **Congo** (c) **Nile** (d) **Yangtze**

Quiz 11 score

History QUIZ

12

Q9

1 What were yurts?
(a) **Magic spells**   (b) **Chinese soldiers**   (c) **Mongol homes**   (d) **Boats**

2 What language did an Italian-born Roman speak?   Q1
(a) **Italian**   (b) **Latin**   (c) **Greek**   (d) **English**

3 What were the *Queen Mary* and *Queen Elizabeth* of the 1930s?
(a) **Ocean liners**   (b) **Racing cars**   (c) **First jet planes**   (d) **New countries**

4 Who went to China and back again?   Q4
(a) **Columbus**   (b) **Marco Polo**   (c) **Saladin**   (d) **Michelangelo**

5 Which ancient civilization created the Hanging Gardens?
(a) **China**   (b) **Cambodia**   (c) **Zimbabwe**   (d) **Babylon**

6 Who of these was not a British prime minister?
(a) **Churchill**   (b) **Thatcher**   (c) **Blair**   (d) **Kennedy**

7 Who lived in a monastery?
(a) **Monkeys**   (b) **Minstrels**   (c) **Monks**   (d) **Crusaders**

8 What is shown in the Bayeux Tapestry pictures?
(a) **Black Death**   (b) **Norman Conquest**   (c) **Armada**   (d) **Fire of London**

9 Who sailed the sea in longships?
(a) **Very tall fishermen**   (b) **Vikings**   (c) **Marines**   (d) **Carib Indians**

10 Which king is said to have burned some cakes?
(a) **Alfred**   (b) **John**   (c) **George I**   (d) **Edward III**

Quiz 12 score

History
QUIZ

13

Q9

 1 Which event happened most recently?
(a) **Moon landing**   (b) **D-Day**   (c) **Crimean War**   (d) **Fall of the Berlin Wall**

 2 Norsemen is another name for … who?
(a) **Normans**   (b) **Maori**   (c) **Inuit**   (d) **Vikings**

 3 What number in the 'Louis list' was Louis XIV of France?
(a) **5th**   (b) **10th**   (c) **14th**   (d) **21st**

Q2

 4 Where did Catherine the Great rule in the 1700s?
(a) **Russia**   (b) **Sweden**   (c) **France**   (d) **Spain**

 5 Where was the Mughal or Mogul empire?
(a) **South America**   (b) **West Africa**   (c) **India**   (d) **Southeast Asia**

 6 Born in 1890, died in 1962 – how old would this person have been?
(a) **62**   (b) **82**   (c) **72**   (d) **90**

 7 Which is oldest?
(a) **Great Pyramid**   (b) **Tower of London**   (c) **Hadrian's Wall**   (d) **Eiffel Tower**

 8 Which date is in the 1st century BC?
(a) **AD37** (b) **27BC**   (c) **137BC**   (d) **AD110**

Q10

 9 In which war was the Battle of the Somme?
(a) **World War II**   (b) **World War I**   (c) **Crimea**   (d) **Napoleonic Wars**

 10 Which of these was an axe-like club used by North American Indians?
(a) **Tomahawk**   (b) **Mace**   (c) **Musket**   (d) **Grenade**

Quiz 13 score

History QUIZ

14

Q6

 1 Where was Botany Bay, settled by Britain in 1788?
(a) **Canada**   (b) **South Africa**   (c) **Australia**   (d) **New Zealand**

 2 Which was the fighting Scottish king?
(a) **Robert Curthose**   (b) **Robert the Bruce**   (c) **Robert Burns**   (d) **Robert Louis Stevenson**

 3 Which American president could watch himself in old films?
(a) **Ronald Reagan**   (b) **George W. Bush**   (c) **Bill Clinton**   (d) **Teddy Roosevelt**

 4 Where did Magellan's men go between 1519 and 1522?
(a) **The Moon**   (b) **America**   (c) **Around the world**   (d) **Jail**

 5 Where was Thomas Becket killed in 1170?
(a) **Crusades**   (b) **Paris**   (c) **Canterbury**   (d) **Edinburgh**

Q5

 6 Who lost his head in 1649?
(a) **Cromwell**   (b) **Milton**   (c) **Newton**   (d) **Charles I**

 7 Which of these opened in 1869?
(a) **Crystal Palace**   (b) **Heathrow**   (c) **M6**   (d) **Suez Canal**

 8 Who ruled the Ottoman Empire?
(a) **Moroccans**   (b) **Maoris**   (c) **Incas**   (d) **Turks**

 9 What person would have used a flint hand axe?
(a) **Roman**   (b) **Tudor**   (c) **Stone Age**   (d) **Victorian**   Q9

 10 Which of these peoples did not invade the British Isles?
(a) **Celts**   (b) **Saxons**   (c) **Mongols**   (d) **Vikings**

Quiz 14 score

History QUIZ

15

Q5

1 Which came down in 1989?
(a) **Sputnik 1** (b) **Berlin Wall** (c) **London Bridge** (d) **Leaning Tower of Pisa**

2 Which of these was a military alliance formed in the 1940s?
(a) **UN** (b) **WWF** (c) **NATO** (d) **ITN**

3 Where did a civil war last from 1936 to 1939?
(a) **France** (b) **Mexico** (c) **Spain** (d) **Greece**

Q4

4 Which British admiral died on board HMS *Victory*?
(a) **Drake** (b) **Beattie** (c) **Nelson** (d) **Grenville**

5 What animal helped spread the Black Death?
(a) **Pigeon** (b) **Rat** (c) **Spider** (d) **Bat**

6 To which land did Crusaders travel in the Middle Ages?
(a) **Holy Land** (b) **Promised Land** (c) **Newfoundland** (d) **Greenland**

7 What did a trebuchet do?
(a) **Send messages** (b) **Hurl rocks** (c) **Torture prisoners** (d) **Cook food**

8 Where did the Toltecs live?
(a) **Canada** (b) **Pakistan** (c) **Mexico** (d) **Egypt**

Q8

9 Which country was ruled by the Ming emperors?
(a) **Japan** (b) **China** (c) **Hawaii** (d) **Sri Lanka**

10 Where are the remains of Great Zimbabwe?
(a) **America** (b) **Africa** (c) **Asia** (d) **Europe**

Quiz 15 score

History QUIZ

16

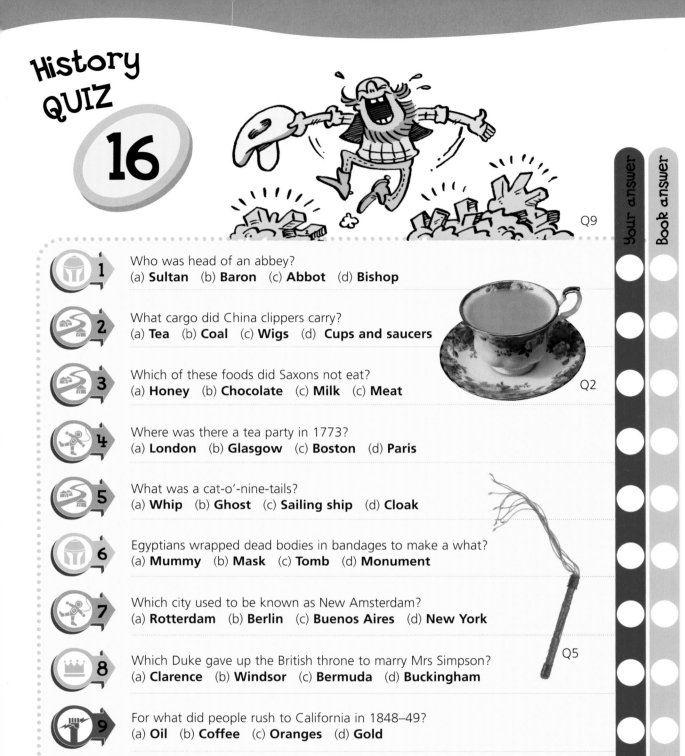

Q9

1. Who was head of an abbey?
   (a) **Sultan** (b) **Baron** (c) **Abbot** (d) **Bishop**

2. What cargo did China clippers carry?
   (a) **Tea** (b) **Coal** (c) **Wigs** (d) **Cups and saucers**

   Q2

3. Which of these foods did Saxons not eat?
   (a) **Honey** (b) **Chocolate** (c) **Milk** (c) **Meat**

4. Where was there a tea party in 1773?
   (a) **London** (b) **Glasgow** (c) **Boston** (d) **Paris**

5. What was a cat-o'-nine-tails?
   (a) **Whip** (b) **Ghost** (c) **Sailing ship** (d) **Cloak**

6. Egyptians wrapped dead bodies in bandages to make a what?
   (a) **Mummy** (b) **Mask** (c) **Tomb** (d) **Monument**

7. Which city used to be known as New Amsterdam?
   (a) **Rotterdam** (b) **Berlin** (c) **Buenos Aires** (d) **New York**

   Q5

8. Which Duke gave up the British throne to marry Mrs Simpson?
   (a) **Clarence** (b) **Windsor** (c) **Bermuda** (d) **Buckingham**

9. For what did people rush to California in 1848–49?
   (a) **Oil** (b) **Coffee** (c) **Oranges** (d) **Gold**

10. Of which country was Mrs Meir prime minister?
    (a) **Russia** (b) **Israel** (c) **Sri Lanka** (d) **India**

Your answer

Book answer

Quiz 16 score

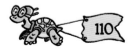

History QUIZ

17

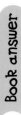

1 In which century was the Thirty Years War?
(a) **17th** (b) **15th** (c) **19th** (d) **12th**

2 Which of these was a kind of cannon?
(a) **Culvert** (b) **Culpepper** (c) **Culverin** (d) **Cul-de-sac**

Q5

3 King Richard I's nickname was…what?
(a) **Braveheart** (b) **Lionheart** (c) **Stoutheart** (d) **Faintheart**

4 Which name means 'southern ape'?
(a) **Homo sapiens** (b) **Cro-Magnon** (c) **Australopithecus** (d) **Neanderthal**

5 In which country was the Taj Mahal built?
(a) **China** (b) **Turkey** (c) **India** (d) **Persia**

6 In which century was the Battle of Waterloo (1815)?
(a) **17th** (b) **18th** (c) **19th** (d) **20th**

7 Which country had prohibition (no drinking) laws in the 1920s?
(a) **Saudi Arabia** (b) **USA** (c) **Britain** (d) **Australia**

Q8

8 What was a privateer?
(a) **Con-man** (b) **Shopkeeper** (c) **Pirate** (d) **Doctor**

9 Which modern sports festival dates from 1896?
(a) **World Cup** (b) **Wimbledon** (c) **Olympic Games** (d) **Test cricket**

10 What game was Francis Drake playing in 1588?
(a) **Cricket** (b) **Bowls** (c) **Cards** (d) **Pool**

Quiz 17 score

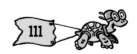

History QUIZ

18

Q5

| | Your answer | Book answer |

1 Which ancient statue has a lion's body and a human head
(a) **Pyx**   (b) **Sphinx**   (c) **Colossus**   (d) **Phalanx**

2 Which of these was a British prime minister?
(a) **Palmerston**   (b) **Chaplin**   (c) **Lynam**   (d) **Gallagher**

Q1

3 Which building has a moat and drawbridge?
(a) **Cathedral**   (b) **Castle**   (c) **Dungeon**   (d) **Palace**

4 Where did Napoleon die?
(a) **St Helena**   (b) **Tower of London**   (c) **Bastille**   (d) **America**

5 Who was the notorious bank robber?
(a) **Colonel Custer**   (b) **Crazy Horse**   (c) **General Grant**   (d) **Jesse James**

6 Of which country was Malcolm Canmore king?
(a) **Ireland**   (b) **Scotland**   (c) **Wales**   (d) **England**

7 Which is not an English 'royal house'?
(a) **Plantagenet**   (b) **Tudor**   (c) **Bourbon**   (d) **Windsor**

8 What killed Cleopatra?
(a) **Arrow**   (b) **Snake**   (c) **Illness**   (d) **Meteorite**

Q10

9 Which scientist knew about gravity in 1665?
(a) **Einstein**   (b) **Edison**   (c) **Faraday**   (d) **Newton**

10 Where was Jomo Kenyatta president in 1964?
(a) **USA**   (b) **New Zealand**   (c) **Kenya**   (d) **South Africa**

Quiz 18 score

History QUIZ

19

Q5

 1 Who led a Grand Army into Russia in 1812?
(a) **Hannibal**   (b) **Hitler**   (c) **Genghis Khan**   (d) **Napoleon**

 2 Which invention made things brighter in the 1870s?
(a) **TV**   (b) **Cinema**   (c) **Light bulb**   (d) **Candle**

Q2

 3 Which revolutionary wrote *The Little Red Book*?
(a) **Hans Andersen**   (b) **Mao Zedong**   (c) **Stalin**   (d) **Washington**

 4 Which of these battles was fought at sea?
(a) **Agincourt**   (b) **Jutland**   (c) **Blenheim**   (d) **Naseby**

 5 Which was a nickname for a British soldier?
(a) **Blackshirt**   (b) **Greenhat**   (c) **Yellowsocks**   (d) **Redcoat**

 6 Which explorer never went to Africa?
(a) **Daniel Boone**   (b) **Mungo Park**   (c) **Henry Stanley**   (d) **Richard Burton**

 7 What was dynamite, invented in 1866?
(a) **Plastic**   (b) **Explosive**   (c) **Chewing gum**   (d) **Breakfast cereal**

 8 What was a Victorian penny dreadful?
(a) **Sweet**   (b) **Public toilet**   (c) **Short film**   (d) **Magazine**

 9 Who was not a Saxon king?
(a) **Edgar**   (b) **Athelstan**   (c) **John**   (d) **Alfred**

Q6

 10 In which decade did World War II start?
(a) **1920s**   (b) **1930s**   (c) **1940s**   (d) **1950s**

Quiz 19 score

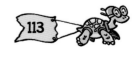

History QUIZ

20

Q9

 1 Which person was not a painter?
(a) **Tolstoy**   (b) **Reynolds**   (c) **Goya**   (d) **Monet**

 2 Which of these people saw the Spanish Armada?
(a) **Nelson**   (b) **Drake**   (c) **Churchill**   (d) **Wellington**

Q2

 3 Why do we wear poppies in November?
(a) **Remembrance**   (b) **Halloween**   (c) **Guy Fawkes**   (d) **Russian Revolution**

 4 What year would be the 50th anniversary of 1960?
(a) **2010**   (b) **2000**   (c) **1965**   (d) **1910**

 5 Which of these rescued Victorian street-children?
(a) **Dr Jekyll**   (b) **Dr Johnson**   (c) **Dr Spock**   (d) **Dr Barnardo**

 6 What name was given to German air attacks in World War II?
(a) **Armageddon**   (b) **D-Day**   (c) **Blitz**   (d) **Judgement Day**

 7 Which engineer designed steam trains?
(a) **Brunel**   (b) **Arkwright**   (c) **Telford**   (d) **Stephenson**

 8 Find the British prime minister?
(a) **Lloyd George**   (b) **Livingstone**   (c) **Attenborough**   (d) **Orwell**

Q8

 9 Which queen had her head cut off?
(a) **Elizabeth I**   (b) **Mary I**   (c) **Anne**   (d) **Mary Queen of Scots**

 10 Which means 'furthest back' in history?
(a) **Now**   (b) **Recently**   (c) **Centuries ago**   (d) **In future**

Quiz 20 score

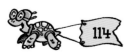

History QUIZ

21

Q10

| | Your answer | Book answer |

1 Which country had the greatest Great Wall?
(a) **Scotland**   (b) **Germany**   (c) **India**   (d) **China**

2 Who is remembered on Bonfire Night?
(a) **Hitler**   (b) **Guy Fawkes**   (c) **Henry VIII**   (d) **Robin Hood**

3 Who built a 'lost city' named Machu Picchu?
(a) **Inuit**   (b) **Vikings**   (c) **Romans**   (d) **Incas**

Q4

4 Which Scottish hero was known as Braveheart?
(a) **Bruce**   (b) **Knox**   (c) **Wallace**   (d) **Balliol**

5 Which of these was set up in 1948 in Britain?
(a) **Internet**   (b) **Premiership**   (c) **National Health Service**   (d) **BBC**

6 Which town became a seaside resort in the late 1700s?
(a) **Newcastle**   (b) **Cardiff**   (c) **Liverpool**   (d) **Brighton**

7 In which country did Owen Glendower lead a revolt?
(a) **Ireland**   (b) **Scotland**   (c) **Wales**   (d) **England**

Q10

8 Which emperor set out for Britain in AD43?
(a) **Kublai Khan**   (b) **Napoleon**   (c) **Claudius**   (d) **Nero**

9 In which river valley was the city of Mohenjo-Daro?
(a) **Thames**   (b) **Mississippi**   (c) **Indus**   (d) **Nile**

10 Which event occurred first?
(a) **Armada**   (b) **Norman Conquest**   (c) **Trojan War**   (d) **World War I**

Quiz 21 score

History QUIZ

22

Q5

 1 An event 50 years before the birth of Christ happened in…what year?
(a) **150BC** (b) **50BC** (c) **AD50** (d) **500BC**

 2 Where did pharaohs reign?
(a) **China** (b) **Babylon** (c) **Crete** (d) **Egypt**

 3 In which English city was the Jorvik settlement?
(a) **Manchester** (b) **York** (c) **Birmingham** (d) **London**

Q4

 4 Which ancient army had cohorts and centurions?
(a) **Persian** (b) **Greek** (c) **Roman** (d) **Saxon**

 5 Who said: 'England is a nation of shopkeepers'?
(a) **Victoria** (b) **De Gaulle** (c) **Napoleon** (d) **Colonel Sanders**

 6 Which medieval person wore a cap with bells?
(a) **Monk** (b) **Sailor** (c) **Jester** (d) **Priest**

Q8

 7 Which war lasted from 1914 to 1918?
(a) **World War I** (b) **Boer War** (c) **World War II** (d) **Vietnam War**

 8 Who led the 1745 Jacobite uprising?
(a) **Bonnie Prince Charlie** (b) **Rob Roy** (c) **William Wallace** (d) **Robin Hood**

 9 What did Nicolas Cugnot drive in 1769?
(a) **Coach** (b) **Mail train** (c) **Steam carriage** (d) **Electric car**

 10 Which general captured Quebec in 1759?
(a) **Fox** (b) **Wolfe** (c) **Lamb** (d) **Husky**

Quiz 22 score

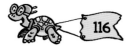

History QUIZ

23

Q5

		Your answer	Book answer

 1 Which battle gave its name to a long race?
(a) **Sluys** (b) **Waterloo** (c) **Marathon** (d) **Edgehill**

 2 Which event happened in 1903?
(a) **First plane flight** (b) **French Revolution** (c) **Black Death** (d) **First TV show**

 3 Who was the first British woman prime minister?
(a) **Mrs Pankhurst** (b) **Mrs Gandhi** (c) **Mrs Thatcher** (d) **Mrs Pitt**

 4 What was the name of the Pilgrims' ship in 1620?
(a) **Wallflower** (b) **Sunflower** (c) **Cauliflower** (d) **Mayflower**

 5 What was a 'prairie schooner' in the American West?
(a) **Canoe** (b) **Tent** (c) **Hat** (d) **Wagon**

Q6

 6 What was Dick Turpin's job?
(a) **Hangman** (b) **Highwayman** (c) **Pirate** (d) **Judge**

 7 Where is El Cid a national hero?
(a) **Australia** (b) **Mexico** (c) **Spain** (d) **Scotland**

 8 Which city had a Forum beside the Tiber?
(a) **Rome** (b) **Delhi** (c) **London** (d) **New York**

Q7

 9 Who kept warm with a hypocaust – underground heating?
(a) **Inuit** (b) **Chinese** (c) **Romans** (d) **Greeks**

 10 In which century was the printing press invented?
(a) **800s** (b) **1400s** (c) **1600s** (d) **1800s**

Quiz 23 score

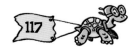

History QUIZ
24

Q2

1 Who or what was a quack?
(a) **Duck-keeper** (b) **Fake doctor** (c) **Highwayman** (d) **Crooked lawyer**

Q3

2 Which US President gave his name to the teddy bear?
(a) **Lincoln** (b) **Roosevelt** (c) **Grant** (d) **Reagan**

3 Who rescued Captain Smith?
(a) **Pocahontas** (b) **Joan of Arc** (c) **Elizabeth I** (d) **Edith Cavell**

4 Where did Fidel Castro lead a revolution in the 1950s?
(a) **Brazil** (b) **Ghana** (c) **Pakistan** (d) **Cuba**

5 Who witnessed the Great Fire of London in 1666?
(a) **Queen Victoria** (b) **Samuel Pepys** (c) **Duke of Edinburgh** (d) **Charles Dickens**

6 Where was the 1916 Easter Rising?
(a) **Russia** (b) **China** (c) **Spain** (d) **Ireland**

7 Which Johnson was a famous flier?
(a) **Lyndon** (b) **Samuel** (c) **Jack** (d) **Amy**

Q8

8 Who wrote in hieroglyphics?
(a) **Spies** (b) **Egyptians** (c) **Chinese** (d) **Cretans**

9 Cyrus and Darius were kings…where?
(a) **Persia** (b) **Greece** (c) **Assyria** (d) **France**

10 Where did the Khmers rule?
(a) **New Zealand** (b) **Finland** (c) **Cambodia** (d) **China**

Quiz 24 score

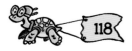

History QUIZ

25

Q7

1 Where was the 19th-century 'workshop of the world'?
(a) **USA**   (b) **Britain**   (c) **Japan**   (d) **Russia**

2 Where did Maoris go in canoes?
(a) **New Zealand**   (b) **India**   (c) **Argentina**   (d) **Canada**

3 Of which people was Shaka a king?
(a) **Saxons**   (b) **Vikings**   (c) **Zulus**   (d) **Incas**

Q2

4 Who fought the American Civil War?
(a) **Greeks/Romans**   (b) **Reds/Whites**   (c) **Confederacy/Union**   (d) **Celts/Vikings**

5 Who was Britain's first Stuart monarch?
(a) **William I**   (b) **Henry I**   (c) **James I**   (d) **George I**

6 Of which country was Kemal Ataturk the modern founder?
(a) **Egypt**   (b) **Iraq**   (c) **Turkey**   (d) **Libya**

7 What was Drake's *Pelican*?
(a) **Pet bird**   (b) **Secret society**   (c) **Inn**   (d) **Ship**

Q10

8 Which of these queens reigned longest?
(a) **Mary I**   (b) **Anne**   (c) **Victoria**   (d) **Elizabeth I**

9 Where did Pizarro conquer in the 1530s?
(a) **Canada**   (b) **Peru**   (c) **China**   (d) **Nigeria**

10 Who was Edward III's warrior-son?
(a) **White Knight**   (b) **Hotspur**   (c) **Black Prince**   (d) **Green Knight**

Quiz 25 score

History QUIZ

26

Q4

 1 Where is Garibaldi a national hero?
(a) **Afghanistan** (b) **France** (c) **Italy** (d) **Greece**

Q8

 2 Where was Frederick the Great King in the 1700s?
(a) **Britain** (b) **France** (c) **USA** (d) **Prussia**

 3 Where did Mary Seacole look after soldiers?
(a) **North Pole** (b) **Crimea** (c) **South Africa** (d) **America**

 4 Who crossed the Alps with elephants?
(a) **Hengist** (b) **Harold** (c) **Hardicanute** (d) **Hannibal**

 5 Which king sat on a beach and told the waves to stop?
(a) **Cnut** (b) **Alfred** (c) **Arthur** (d) **Henry VIII**

 6 Who led the 1917 Revolution in Russia?
(a) **Lenin** (b) **Putin** (c) **Yeltsin** (d) **Nicholas**

Q5

 7 Where was Kwame Nkrumah president in 1960?
(a) **South Africa** (b) **Ghana** (c) **Germany** (d) **USA**

 8 Which Roman emperor saw his city burn?
(a) **Claudius** (b) **Constantine** (c) **Hadrian** (d) **Nero**

 9 Who sailed the ocean blue in 1492?
(a) **Columbus** (b) **Darwin** (c) **Magellan** (d) **Anson**

 10 Who was murdered in Rome in 44BC?
(a) **Mussolini** (b) **Julius Caesar** (c) **Pontius Pilate** (d) **St Paul**

Quiz 26 score

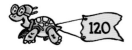

History QUIZ

27

Q5

 1 Who founded the Methodist Church in the 1700s?
(a) **John Peel** (b) **John Wesley** (c) **John O'Groats** (d) **John Bull**

 2 What kind of machines were the R-34 and Hindenburg?
(a) **Ships** (b) **Submarines** (c) **Rockets** (d) **Airships**

Q2

 3 What was a barbican?
(a) **Part of a castle** (b) **Armour suit** (c) **Part of a horse** (d) **Kind of archer**

 4 What was the old name for Iran?
(a) **Abyssinia** (b) **Cathay** (c) **Muscovy** (d) **Persia**

 5 What happened to a sheep, chicken and duck in 1783?
(a) **Flew in a balloon** (b) **Rode in a car** (c) **Travelled by train** (d) **Flew in space**

 6 Who was Lord Darnley's queenly wife?
(a) **Victoria** (b) **Mary Queen of Scots** (c) **Elizabeth I** (d) **Anne Boleyn**

 7 Which king ordered Domesday Book to be made in 1086?
(a) **Alfred the Great** (b) **William I** (c) **Henry II** (d) **Edward I**

 8 Where did Burke and Wills walk across the desert?
(a) **Africa** (b) **Australia** (c) **America** (d) **Asia**

Q10

 9 What was the title of the Russian emperor?
(a) **Shah** (b) **Czar** (c) **Caesar** (d) **Imperator**

 10 Which was the British warrior-queen?
(a) **Jezebel** (b) **Delilah** (c) **Boudicca** (d) **Ethel**

Quiz 27 score

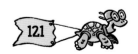

History QUIZ

28

Q9

| | | Your answer | Book answer |

1 Which of these 20th-century battles was fought in a desert?
(a) **El Alamein**   (b) **Coral Sea**   (c) **Stalingrad**   (d) **Atlantic**

2 Which event could someone born in 1900 not have seen?
(a) **First plane flight** (b) **First TV** (c) **First Moon landing** (d) **First steam train**

3 Which English city was named Londinium by the Romans?
(a) **Lincoln**   (b) **Dover**   (c) **London**   (d) **Colchester**

4 Who in the Bible killed Goliath?
(a) **David**   (b) **Samson**   (c) **Solomon**   (d) **Joseph**   Q3

5 Where was there a great Rebellion or Mutiny in 1857?
(a) **India**   (b) **Russia**   (c) **France**   (d) **China**

6 Which language did Aristotle and Plato speak?
(a) **Chinese**   (b) **French**   (c) **Greek**   (d) **English**

7 Which of these people kept a famous diary?
(a) **Shakespeare**   (b) **Pepys**   (c) **Newton**   (d) **Cromwell**

Q6

8 Which of these came into use the longest time ago?
(a) **Internet**   (b) **Telephone**   (c) **Telegraph**   (d) **Watermill**

9 Which of these is known to have been a real person?
(a) **Robin Hood**   (b) **Davy Crockett**   (c) **Lancelot of the Lake**   (d) **Romulus**

10 Which of these was not an ancient Egyptian?
(a) **Tutankhamen**   (b) **Nefertiti**   (c) **Agamemnon**   (d) **Akenaten**

Quiz 28 score

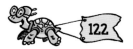

Chart Your Scores

History	1	2	3	4	5	6	7	8	9	10
Quiz 1										
Quiz 2										
Quiz 3										
Quiz 4										
Quiz 5										
Quiz 6										
Quiz 7										
Quiz 8										
Quiz 9										
Quiz 10										
Quiz 11										
Quiz 12										
Quiz 13										
Quiz 14										
Quiz 15										
Quiz 16										
Quiz 17										
Quiz 18										
Quiz 19										
Quiz 20										
Quiz 21										
Quiz 22										
Quiz 23										
Quiz 24										
Quiz 25										
Quiz 26										
Quiz 27										
Quiz 28										

English Answers

Quiz 1
1b, 2a, 3a, 4b, 5a, 6b, 7c, 8a, 9a, 10c

Quiz 2
1b, 2c, 3a, 4a, 5c, 6d, 7b, 8a, 9d, 10a

Quiz 3
1a, 2d, 3a, 4a, 5a, 6b, 7d, 8b, 9c, 10c

Quiz 4
1a, 2c, 3a, 4b, 5a, 6b, 7d, 8a, 9b, 10a

Quiz 5
1a, 2c, 3b, 4a, 5d, 6b, 7c, 8c, 9b, 10a

Quiz 6
1a, 2d, 3a, 4a, 5d, 6b, 7d, 8c, 9d, 10a

Quiz 7
1c, 2c, 3a, 4d, 5c, 6d, 7b, 8c, 9a, 10d

Quiz 8
1b, 2a, 3b, 4a, 5c, 6a, 7a, 8d, 9c, 10a

Quiz 9
1d, 2b, 3d, 4d, 5a, 6c, 7a, 8c, 9b, 10c

Quiz 10
1b, 2c, 3b, 4c, 5c, 6b, 7a, 8d, 9a, 10c

Quiz 11
1b, 2d, 3a, 4c, 5b, 6b, 7b, 8d, 9a, 10d

Quiz 12
1d, 2b, 3d, 4b, 5a, 6a, 7b, 8c, 9a, 10b

Quiz 13
1a, 2b, 3b, 4a, 5d, 6d, 7b, 8c, 9b, 10a

Quiz 14
1b, 2c, 3c, 4c, 5b, 6c, 7c, 8a, 9c, 10b

Quiz 15
1d, 2a, 3c, 4c, 5a, 6a, 7b, 8c, 9a, 10b

Quiz 16
1c, 2b, 3d, 4a, 5a, 6b, 7d, 8c, 9b, 10b

Quiz 17
1b, 2c, 3a, 4b, 5b, 6a, 7b, 8a, 9c, 10b

Quiz 18
1c, 2b, 3b, 4d, 5c, 6b, 7a, 8b, 9a, 10a

Quiz 19
1a, 2b, 3d, 4a, 5a, 6d, 7a, 8a, 9c, 10a

Quiz 20
1a, 2a, 3c, 4b, 5c, 6b, 7c, 8a, 9b, 10d

Quiz 21
1d, 2c, 3b, 4a, 5a, 6b, 7a, 8b, 9d, 10b

Quiz 22
1b, 2a, 3c, 4c, 5c, 6a, 7c, 8a, 9a, 10d

Quiz 23
1c, 2d, 3c, 4a, 5a, 6d, 7d, 8c, 9d, 10b

Quiz 24
1b, 2a, 3b, 4b, 5b, 6a, 7b, 8d, 9b, 10a

Quiz 25
1b, 2c, 3a, 4b, 5c, 6d, 7a, 8a, 9b, 10d

Quiz 26
1d, 2d, 3c, 4d, 5d, 6a, 7c, 8d, 9b, 10b

Quiz 27
1b, 2b, 3b, 4a, 5d, 6b, 7c, 8b, 9a, 10a

Quiz 28
1d, 2a, 3a, 4b, 5c, 6b, 7c, 8c, 9c, 10c

Maths Answers

Quiz 1
1a, 2d, 3a, 4c, 5a, 6b, 7b, 8a, 9d, 10a

Quiz 2
1b, 2b, 3c, 4d, 5b, 6a, 7b, 8b, 9a, 10c

Quiz 3
1c, 2d, 3a, 4d, 5b, 6c, 7c, 8a, 9b, 10c

Quiz 4
1d, 2a, 3c, 4c, 5a, 6c, 7a, 8d, 9a, 10d

Quiz 5
1b, 2a, 3b, 4c, 5c, 6b, 7c, 8b, 9c, 10c

Quiz 6
1a, 2b, 3b, 4a, 5c, 6c, 7b, 8a, 9c, 10b

Quiz 7
1d, 2a, 3a, 4a, 5a, 6b, 7a, 8a, 9b, 10b

Quiz 8
1b, 2b, 3c, 4b, 5a, 6b, 7b, 8c, 9c, 10d

Quiz 9
1b, 2c, 3a, 4c, 5b, 6d, 7a, 8c, 9a, 10c

Quiz 10
1d, 2d, 3c, 4b, 5b, 6a, 7b, 8d, 9c, 10a

Quiz 11
1c, 2a, 3b, 4b, 5b, 6c, 7a, 8a, 9c, 10a

Quiz 12
1a, 2b, 3c, 4c, 5b, 6a, 7b, 8d, 9b, 10c

Quiz 13
1b, 2a, 3d, 4c, 5a, 6c, 7c, 8b, 9a, 10b

Quiz 14
1b, 2a, 3b, 4b, 5a, 6c, 7b, 8a, 9b, 10b

Quiz 15
1b, 2d, 3b, 4a, 5d, 6c, 7c, 8a, 9a, 10b

Quiz 16
1a, 2b, 3c, 4a, 5c, 6b, 7d, 8a, 9c, 10d

Quiz 17
1b, 2c, 3b, 4a, 5c, 6b, 7d, 8c, 9a, 10d

Quiz 18
1c, 2b, 3d, 4a, 5a, 6b, 7b, 8b, 9a, 10b

Quiz 19
1b, 2c, 3b, 4c, 5c, 6b, 7b, 8a , 9b, 10c

Quiz 20
1b, 2a, 3a, 4b, 5d, 6d, 7b, 8d, 9b, 10a

Quiz 21
1c, 2a, 3b, 4c, 5b, 6c, 7a, 8c, 9c, 10b

Quiz 22
1d, 2a, 3c, 4d, 5b, 6d, 7c, 8c, 9b, 10b

Quiz 23
1b, 2c, 3a, 4c, 5b, 6b, 7d, 8d, 9c, 10d

Quiz 24
1b, 2b, 3c, 4d, 5c, 6c, 7a, 8a, 9b, 10b

Quiz 25
1a, 2b, 3b, 4c, 5a, 6b, 7c, 8a, 9a, 10a

Quiz 26
1c, 2a, 3c, 4b, 5b, 6b, 7c, 8d, 9d, 10a

Quiz 27
1a, 2b, 3c, 4a, 5a, 6b, 7b, 8a, 9d, 10a

Quiz 28
1a, 2b, 3c, 4c, 5c, 6d, 7a, 8a, 9c, 10b

Science Answers

Quiz 1
1a, 2c, 3d, 4a, 5c, 6a, 7c, 8d, 9c, 10b

Quiz 2
1d, 2a, 3b, 4c, 5d, 6a, 7b, 8a, 9b, 10a

Quiz 3
1a, 2d, 3a, 4d, 5b, 6b, 7a, 8b, 9c, 10d

Quiz 4
1a, 2b, 3b, 4a, 5b, 6b, 7c, 8d, 9a, 10b

Quiz 5
1b, 2b, 3c, 4c, 5a, 6c, 7d, 8d, 9c, 10b

Quiz 6
1a, 2b, 3c, 4b, 5a, 6c, 7d, 8b, 9d, 10d

Quiz 7
1b, 2d, 3a, 4c, 5b, 6a, 7a, 8a, 9d, 10c

Quiz 8
1b, 2c, 3d, 4d, 5c, 6d, 7b, 8a, 9d, 10a

Quiz 9
1d, 2c, 3b, 4d, 5a, 6d, 7d, 8a, 9a, 10b

Quiz 10
1a, 2b, 3a, 4d, 5c, 6b, 7a, 8b, 9b, 10d

Quiz 11
1a, 2b, 3d, 4c, 5b, 6d, 7c, 8c, 9a, 10b

Quiz 12
1d, 2a, 3b, 4a, 5c, 6d, 7a, 8b, 9c, 10d

Quiz 13
1b, 2c, 3b, 4a, 5b, 6d, 7a, 8d, 9b, 10b

Quiz 14
1c, 2b, 3c, 4b, 5a, 6c, 7b, 8c, 9c, 10b

Quiz 15
1a, 2c, 3a, 4a, 5d, 6d, 7b, 8b, 9a, 10c

Quiz 16
1c, 2d, 3a, 4b, 5b, 6c, 7c, 8a, 9b, 10d

Quiz 17
1c, 2c, 3d, 4b, 5b, 6b, 7d, 8a, 9b, 10a

Quiz 18
1c, 2d, 3c, 4b, 5c, 6c, 7d, 8d, 9a, 10b

Quiz 19
1a, 2b, 3c, 4d, 5c, 6b, 7a, 8d, 9c, 10d

Quiz 20
1d, 2d, 3b, 4d, 5b, 6d, 7a, 8c, 9b, 10c

Quiz 21
1d, 2b, 3c, 4d, 5b, 6a, 7d, 8c, 9d, 10d

Quiz 22
1d, 2b, 3b, 4c, 5a, 6b, 7d, 8c, 9a, 10a

Quiz 23
1c, 2d, 3a, 4b, 5b, 6b, 7b, 8b, 9a, 10d

Quiz 24
1b, 2b, 3c, 4c, 5a, 6a, 7c, 8c, 9b, 10d

Quiz 25
1b, 2c, 3b, 4d, 5c, 6d, 7d, 8b, 9d, 10a

Quiz 26
1b, 2a, 3c, 4b, 5d, 6b, 7b, 8c, 9b, 10b

Quiz 27
1d, 2a, 3c, 4b, 5d, 6d, 7a, 8a, 9b, 10c

Quiz 28
1c, 2a, 3c, 4b, 5d, 6c, 7a, 8b, 9a, 10b